New Mexico's Struggle for Statehood

New Mexico's Struggle for Statehood

Sixty Years of Effort to Obtain Self-Government

Facsimile of 1910 Edition

by
L. Bradford Prince

New Foreword
by
Richard Melzer, PhD

SANTA FE

New Material © 2010 by Sunstone Press. All Rights Reserved.

No part of this book may be reproduced in any form or by any electronic or mechanical means including information storage and retrieval systems without permission in writing from the publisher, except by a reviewer who may quote brief passages in a review.

Sunstone books may be purchased for educational, business, or sales promotional use. For information please write: Special Markets Department, Sunstone Press, P.O. Box 2321, Santa Fe, New Mexico 87504-2321.

Library of Congress Cataloging-in-Publication Data

Prince, L. Bradford (Le Baron Bradford), 1840-1922.
  New Mexico's struggle for statehood : sixty years of effort to obtain self-government / by L. Bradford Prince ; new foreword by Richard Melzer.
    p. cm. -- (Southwest heritage series)
  "Facsimile of 1910 edition."
  Originally published: Santa Fe : New Mexican Print. Co., 1910.
  With new foreword.
  Includes bibliographical references.
  ISBN 978-0-86534-731-1 (softcover : alk. paper)
  1. New Mexico--Politics and government--1848-1950.
  2. New Mexico--History--1848- I. Title.
  F801.P82 2010
  978.9--dc22
                              2010001876

WWW.SUNSTONEPRESS.COM
SUNSTONE PRESS / POST OFFICE BOX 2321 / SANTA FE, NM 87504-2321 /USA
(505) 988-4418 / ORDERS ONLY (800) 243-5644 / FAX (505) 988-1025

CONTENTS

I
THE SOUTHWEST HERITAGE SERIES

II
FOREWORD TO THIS EDITION

III
BIOGRAPHICAL SKETCH

IV
IN MEMORY OF L. BRADFORD PRINCE
Historical Society of New Mexico

V
FACSIMILE OF 1910 EDITION

SOUTHWEST HERITAGE SERIES

I

THE SOUTHWEST HERITAGE SERIES

> "The past is not dead. In fact, it's not even past."
> —William Faulkner, *Requiem for a Nun*

The history of the United States is written in hundreds of regional histories and literary works. Those letters, essays, memoirs, biographies and even collections of fiction are often first-hand accounts by people who wanted to memorialize an event, a person or simply record for posterity the concerns and issues of the times. Many of these accounts have been lost, destroyed or overlooked. Some are in private or public collections but deemed to be in too fragile condition to permit handling by contemporary readers and researchers.

However, now with the application of twenty-first century technology, nineteenth and twentieth century material can be reprinted and made accessible to the general public. These early writings are the DNA of our history and culture and are essential to understanding the present in terms of the past.

The Southwest Heritage Series is a form of literary preservation. Heritage by definition implies legacy and these early works are our legacy from those who have gone before us. To properly present and preserve that legacy, no changes in style or contents have been made. The material reprinted stands on its own as it first appeared. The point of view is that of the author and the era in which he or she lived. We would not expect photographs of people from the past to be re-imaged with modern clothes, hair styles and backgrounds. We should not, therefore, expect their ideas and personal philosophies to reflect our modern concepts.

Remember, reading their words and sharing their thoughts is a passport back into understanding how the past was shaped and how it influenced today's world.

Our hope is that new access to these older books will provide readers with a challenging and exciting experience.

II

FOREWORD TO THIS EDITION
by
Richard Melzer, PhD

LeBaron Bradford Prince (1840–1922) was a transplanted New Yorker, a tireless judge, a controversial territorial governor, a gentleman scholar, and an early leader of the Historical Society of New Mexico. In all these roles, and others, he was a passionate advocate of New Mexico statehood. In the words of Robert W. Larson, the foremost authority on the struggle for New Mexico statehood, Prince displayed a readiness "to plunge into the statehood fray" whenever and wherever he was needed.

Prince was born, raised, and educated in New York. As a young attorney, his political career in state politics had progressed well until he clashed with leaders of the state Republican Party machine, led by Roscoe Conkling. Salvaging his political fortunes in the West, Prince won appointment as the chief justice of the New Mexico Supreme Court in 1879. By all accounts, no territorial judge worked harder than Prince, often hearing cases from 8:00 in the morning till 11:00 at night. In what time remained in his busy days, Prince compiled a 603-page volume of territorial laws and began to write history with the clear purpose of advocating New Mexico statehood. His first work on New Mexico history, entitled *Historical Sketches of New Mexico: From the Earliest Records to the American Occupation*, appeared in 1883.

After actively lobbying for the coveted position, Prince won appointment as the thirteenth U.S. territorial governor of New Mexico. Unfortunately, his four-year term in office, 1889-93, was marred by property violence (by the *Gorras Blancas*), political violence (by and against the Santa Fe Ring), and almost continuous political controversy. Despite this turmoil, Prince and his wife Mary were known for their generous hospitality at the Palace of the Governors, sparing little to entertain visitors of all social classes.

In relation to his overriding political goal, Prince convened a state constitutional convention shortly after he entered the governor's office. Knowing that the writing of a state constitution was a major step toward statehood, the governor praised the convention's work as "excellent" but blamed his uncompromising Democratic opponents for the draft's decisive defeat at the polls. In 1890 Prince led a delegation of twenty-nine territorial leaders on a trip to Washington, D.C., to lobby for statehood, among other pressing issues. Unfortunately, the sojourn east proved as futile as the drive to pass an acceptable state constitution.

Once out of office, Prince continued to press for New Mexico statehood, especially through the preservation of the region's long history. Realizing that those outside New Mexico thought of the territory's racial diversity as a disadvantage, Prince argued that each racial group (or at least its leaders) had special qualities that had helped to unite, rather than divide the territory during most of its history. Writing to the editor of the *New York Tribune*, Prince asserted that the sum of these special qualities gave New Mexico "special advantages as a self-governing community over most other Territories" that seemed destined to achieve statehood before New Mexico. These "special advantages" became the major theme of Prince's historical work, whether he was collecting artifacts for the Historical Society of New Mexico, serving as that organization's president and most active member from 1884 to World War I, speaking to civic groups, or writing pertinent history, including *New Mexico's Struggle for Statehood*, published in 1910.

L. Bradford Prince was one of seven territorial governors who attended the January 15th inauguration of New Mexico's first state governor, William C. McDonald, in New Mexico's long-awaited statehood year, 1912. Within a year of that auspicious occasion, Prince published *A Concise History of New Mexico*, a condensation and revision of his *Historical Sketches* of 1883. His purpose in 1913 was to be concise by avoiding the "temptation" to provide excessive historical details, a mild criticism of much longer recent histories by Ralph Emerson Twitchell (five volumes, 1911-17) and Benjamin Read (1912). Prince also hoped that his "little volume" might be of use in the now-required teaching of New Mexico history in the state's public schools. The passage of a public school bill during his term as governor had been considered an important step toward the attainment of statehood. The publication of a state history textbook was meant to be an important contribution to New Mexico public education once statehood had been achieved.

But within a year of its publication, Prince affirmed that the length and price of the already brief *Concise History* was excessive for most public schools and students. While still recommending *A Concise History* for teachers and most adults, Prince offered an even more focused, 174-page work, entitled *The Student's History of New Mexico*.

Now, instead of using history to argue the case for New Mexico statehood, Prince's chief goal was to use history to help create pride in New Mexico for the "clear-eyed, pure hearted, noble minded youth" of the nation's newest state. These future citizens could take pride in both their past, "the most interesting of all American state histories," and in the special qualities of individual groups whose collective story was "unrivaled in ancient or modern times." Proud students would hopefully grow to become good citizens, well prepared to contribute to the making of a strong, modern state. Convinced that *The Student's History* had served its purpose well, Prince later updated his book with an additional ten pages about New Mexico's first few years of statehood. This second edition of *The Student's History* appeared in 1921, a year before Prince's death.

Despite its brevity, *The Student's History* reflects much about Prince and his Anglo generation's thinking about New Mexico and its past, as of the early twentieth century. By our twenty-first century standards, much of this thinking is imperialistic, elitist, and racist. While Prince described most Spanish, Anglo, and Pueblo leaders in appreciative terms and portrayed four of New Mexico's "most noted" Indian fighters with special praise, readers search in vain for references to Navajo or Apache leaders like Geronimo or Cochise, no less for any virtues these Native Americans may have displayed for students to admire and emulate.

The second edition of *The Student's History* is also offered as a brief history of New Mexico of value to the general reader sophisticated enough to recognize its biases, but astute enough to appreciate its many facts. If this unique telling of New Mexico's past adds to our pride in being New Mexicans—or helps others to better understand New Mexico—then L. Bradford Prince will have achieved his purpose long after he departed his beloved New Mexico, once a striving territory and now a productive member of the nation's family of states.

Suggested Readings

Clancey, Frank W. *In Memory of L. Bradford Prince*. Santa Fe: Historical Society of New Mexico, 1923.

Donlon, Walter J. "LeBaron Bradford Prince, Chief Justice and Governor of New Mexico Territory, 1879–1893." Unpublished Ph.D. dissertation, University of New Mexico, 1967.

Lamar, Howard R. *The Far Southwest, 1846–1912: A Territorial History*. Albuquerque: University of New Mexico Press, 2000.

Larson, Robert W. *New Mexico's Quest for Statehood, 1846–1912*. Albuquerque: University of New Mexico Press, 1968.

Montoya, María E. "L. Bradford Prince: The Education of a Gilded Age Politician." *New Mexico Historical Review*, vol. 66 (April 1991): 179–201.

Pattison, J. Michael. "Four 'Gentlemen' Historians of New Mexico." Unpublished M.A. thesis, New Mexico Highlands University, 1992.

Poldervaart, Arie W. *Black-Robed Justice: A History of the Administration of Justice in New Mexico from the American Occupation in 1846 Until Statehood in 1912*. Santa Fe: Historical Society of New Mexico, 1948.

Stensvaag, James T. "Cleo On the Frontier: The Intellectual Evolution of the Historical Society of New Mexico, 1859–1925." *New Mexico Historical Review*, vol. 55 (October 1980): 293–308.

Collected Papers

L. Bradford Prince Papers, Center for Southwest Research, Zimmerman Library, University of New Mexico, Albuquerque, New Mexico.

L. Bradford Prince Papers, New Mexico State Records Center and Archives, Santa Fe, New Mexico.

Main Historical Works by L. Bradford Prince

Prince, L. Bradford. *A Concise History of New Mexico*. Cedar Rapids, Iowa: The Torch Press, 1912.

_____. *Historical Sketches of New Mexico: From the Earliest Records to the American Occupation*. New York: Leggat Brothers, 1883.

_____. *New Mexico's Struggle for Statehood: Sixty Years of Effort to Obtain Self Government*. Santa Fe: New Mexico Printing Company, 1910.

_____. *Spanish Mission Churches of New Mexico*. Santa Fe: Museum of New Mexico Press, 1976; originally published in 1915.

_____. *The Student's History of New Mexico*. Denver: The Publishers Press, 1913; second edition, 1921.

III

BIOGRAPHICAL SKETCH
from
History of New Mexico (1891) by Helen Haines

L. Bradford Prince was born at Flushing (Long Island, New York) on the 3rd of July, 1840. He is a lineal descendant on the maternal side of Governor William Bradford, of Plymouth, one of the "men of the Mayflower," and had for great-grandfather and grandfather respectively Governors Bradford and Collins of Rhode Island. His paternal ancestors are the well-known Prince family of Long Island.

Owing to delicate health much of his early life was passed in the South. As he grew to manhood he engaged in horticultural pursuits at his father's place in Flushing, but after a short experience abandoned this line of employment to study law. Entering Columbia College Law School he passed through the course with special honor, and upon graduating received the $200 prize in political science.

From his youth he was exceedingly active in all matters affecting the welfare and improvement of his native town. In 1858 he originated the Flushing Library Association, obtaining the first subscriptions, drawing its constitution, acting three years as secretary and afterward as president, and from that time until his departure to New Mexico was the leading spirit in all local public affairs.

Very early in life he developed an extraordinary aptitude for political matters, and the activity he displayed in his district during the Frémont campaign won for him a vote of thanks from the town club, of which his age—he was then but a lad of sixteen—prevented his becoming a member. In the canvass of 1860, though still a minor, he was secretary of the local political organization, and worked enthusiastically for the success of the Lincoln ticket. In 1861 he was chosen a member of the Republican county committee of Queens County, on which he served continuously almost twenty years, during several of which he was its secretary and chairman. He was delegate to all State conventions, during the years from 1866 to 1878, with scarcely an exception; was elected a delegate to the National Republican Convention held at Chicago in 1868, which nominated General Grant, and the following year became a member of the State committee. The political labors of Mr. Prince at this period were all the more honorable from the fact that they were pursued merely as a matter of principle, and without the least expectation of personal advancement, the district in which he resided being strongly Democratic. His qualifications for filling a responsible position were, however, too apparent to be neglected, and in 1870 he was elected to the Assembly, members of all parties joining in his support. In 1871 he was re-elected to the Assembly by a large majority, although his opponent was the strongest Democrat in the district and an experienced legislator, who had already served both in the Assembly and in the Senate. The following year he received the extraordinary compliment of a request for his continuance in office, signed by more than two thousand voters, irrespective of party (being a petition over seventy feet long), and, having been nominated by acclamation, was re-elected without opposition. In 1873, having declined a nomination to the Senate, he was again returned to the Assembly without an opposing candidate. In the fall of 1874 the Democrats made a determined effort to redeem the district, which now for four years had been lost to their party, and placed the Honorable Solomon Townsend—who had served three terms in the Legislature and in the constitutional conventions of 1846 and 1867—in opposition to Mr. Prince. The canvass was an exciting one, but resulted in a victory for Mr. Prince, who secured a majority of 771 votes. There is believed to be no other instance on record of a person being elected five successive times in a district politically opposed to him. In the canvass of 1875 Mr. Prince received the Republican nomination for the Senate, and, although the Democrats were successful in the district on the general ticket by nearly 2700 majority, he won the election by a majority of 904, running 3594 ahead of the ticket. The legislative career of Mr. Prince was an exceedingly useful and highly honorable one. In 1872, 1873 and 1874 he was chairman of the judiciary committee, performing the multifarious and arduous duties in the most creditable manner, and rendering valuable service to the State. While filling this position, over 1100 bills came into his hands for reports—a larger number than were ever submitted to any other committee, either State or national, in a similar length of time. During the winter of 1872 it became his duty to conduct the investigation into the official conduct of Judges Barnard, Cardozo, and McCunn. This investigation extended from the middle of February to about the middle of April, during which time 239 witnesses were examined, and over 2400 pages of evidence taken. The thoroughness and fairness with which the investigation was conducted won the approval of fair-minded persons of all shades of political belief, and its results form one of the brightest pages in the history of the recent "reform movement." The reports of the committee in favor of impeaching two of the judges and removing the other met with general public acquiescence, and were adopted by the House, and Mr. Prince was chosen one of the managers to conduct the impeachment trial, receiving 110 out of 113 votes cast on the ballot in the Assembly. He was also appointed to proceed to the bar of the Senate and formally impeach Judge Barnard of high crimes and misdemeanors. He was active in the matter till the close of the trial, and it has been generally conceded that to no other man is the judiciary of the State so much indebted for being relieved of the disgrace that would have attended the retention of Barnard and Cardozo on the bench. The recent amendments to the constitution of the State received from Mr. Prince special attention. In 1872 he introduced, and succeeded in getting passed, the bill for the constitutional commission. During the sessions of 1873 and 1874 he had charge of the proposed amendments, both in committee and in the Assembly, and the task of explaining and defending them fell almost exclusively to his lot. Just previous to these amendments being submitted to the people for ratification—in the fall of 1874—Mr. Prince, at the request of the Council of Political Reform, wrote a pamphlet on the subject, which was widely circulated as a campaign document, and tended largely to their success at the polls. In the session of 1875 he prepared and introduced nearly all the bills required to carry the new constitutional system into effect, that work being assigned to him by general consent, although the Assembly was Democratic.

While in the Legislature Mr. Prince gave special attention to the canal system of the State and the question of transportation from the West to the seaboard. He made several speeches on this subject in the Assembly, as well as at the organization of the Cheap Transportation Association at Cooper Institute in 1874, and at the Produce Exchange meeting in 1875. The New York Chamber of Commerce twice formally acknowledged these services to the mercantile community by votes of thanks. In 1874 he was chairman of the Assembly committee to conduct the United States Senate Committee on Transportation Routes through the State, and performed that duty in September of that year. At different times during 1874 and 1875 he lectured on this subject of transportation in New York, Albany, Troy, Poughkeepsie, etc.

In May, 1876, Mr. Prince was a member of the National Republican Convention which nominated Hayes and Wheeler. In 1877, though tendered a unanimous renomination to the Senate, he declined to serve again, on the ground that he could not afford longer to neglect his private business.

Mr. Prince's reputation is not, however, confined to the field of politics. As a lawyer he occupies a high position, his clear, incisive reasoning power and rare ability as an advocate rendering him eminently successful. In 1868 he was chosen orator of the Alumni Association of the Columbia College Law School, and for two years was president of the association. In 1876, having again been chosen alumni orator, he delivered an oration in the Academy of Music on "The Duties of Citizenship," enforcing the idea that men of character and education should take the lead in political affairs.

Mr. Prince is well known also as a thoughtful writer and lecturer on various topics, among which those relating to legislative and governmental reform have attracted wide attention.

A work from his pen entitled "*E Pluribus Unum*, or American Nationality," a comparison between the Constitution and the Articles of Confederation, passed through several editions in 1868 and received the warmest commendations from statesmen and political scientists. In 1880 a Chicago firm published a work of Mr. Prince's on a somewhat similar subject, entitled "A Nation or a League."

As a speaker he is well known throughout the State, having been active in the general political canvass every year when not himself a candidate, and in 1876 speaking over forty consecutive nights, from Rochester and Salamanca to Plattsburg and Brooklyn.

He is also a prominent member of the Masonic fraternity, having been district deputy grand master of Queens and Suffolk counties for the years 1868, 1869, and 1870, and again in 1876. In 1877 he was appointed on the grand master's staff as grand standard bearer. He is now grand representative of New Mexico to the grand lodge of New York.

Mr. Prince has always taken a very lively interest in all that pertains to the best interests of the farming community, and has delivered a number of addresses before the various agricultural societies throughout the State—more notably those of Saratoga, St. Lawrence, Tioga, Orleans, Suffolk, and Cattaraugus counties. For ten years he was superintendent or director of the Queens County Agricultural Society, and in 1862 wrote an agricultural history of the county, which was published by that society. He is also a life member of the Long Island Historical Society, and for fifteen years—from 1864 to 1879—was an officer in that learned body.

During 1879, without any application or request, Mr. Prince was offered various appointments, including two in foreign countries, the marshalship of New York, the governorship of Idaho, and the chief justiceship of New Mexico. The latter he declined three times, but finally, at the urgent request of Secretary Evarts and the Department of Justice, consented to accept and left for his new home February 1, 1879.

He reached New Mexico on the first Saturday of February and opened court at Santa Fe on the following Monday. The district then embraced all of the territory north of Bernalillo, and before the advent of railroads was a literal "circuit," as the court traveled from county to county in carriages, crossing the Rocky Mountains from Cimarron to Taos and returning to Santa Fe, after many weeks, by way of Rio Arriba. Owing to the influx of population at the opening of the railroad, the business of the district was much larger during the period of Judge Prince's judicial term than ever before or since, but by administrative ability and an extraordinary capacity for work he cleared the docket of old cases and kept abreast of the new business. Great pains were taken by the judge in the selection of the most competent jurors, and the people of the district recognized an absolute impartiality in the court, which they highly appreciated. The first act of the Legislature of 1882 was the passage by a unanimous vote in each house, of resolutions exceedingly complimentary to the chief justice. In May of that year he resigned in order to become a candidate for Congress, but he continued to act as judge until the following August. To show what was accomplished during the three and one half years that he occupied the bench, we quote the following extract from his letter of resignation: "The Court calendars have been cleared of the accumulated business; no less than 1184 civil and 1483 criminal cases have been finally disposed of during the seven circuits which I have held. The critical period surrounding the coming of the first railroad is ended and good order and prosperity everywhere prevail." At the Republican Convention in September, 1882, Judge Prince's nomination was defeated; he generously accepted his defeat, however, and magnanimously moved the unanimous nomination of his opponent; but the party was so highly incensed at the course pursued at the convention, that for the first time in many years a Democratic candidate was elected. In 1884 he was again proposed for nomination and was heartily sustained by the progressive element of the people; at the Territorial convention of that year he was nominated; owing to an opposition ticket having been put in the field, growing out of a political feud in San Miguel County, an election under these circumstances was impossible. Judge Prince, however, made a campaign of wonderful vigor, speaking in all parts of the Territory and resolutely refusing, as the standard bearer of the party, to take any step which would impair the future of Republicans in New Mexico; he received a vote of 9930 against 12,271 for Joseph, and 5792 for Rynerson.

    In 1880 he drew the act for the organization of the Bureau

of Immigration, and when that board organized he was elected President and held that position for a number of years. He was one of the organizers of the Territorial Historical Society in 1880, and in 1882 he was elected president of that society, which position he has held up to the present day and has devoted to this institution much time and attention. In 1881 he was elected President of the University of New Mexico, and has continued to hold that position by successive elections to the present day. When the Tertio Millennial Celebration was organized in 1882 he was elected first vice-president, and in that position worked actively for the success of that wonderful exhibition until its close in August, 1883. He was at one time president of the Santa Fe Board of Trade, and in 1887 he was chosen presiding officer of "The United Miners of New Mexico," a territorial mining organization. Through all this period he was the enthusiastic friend and advocate of his adopted home, and by addresses when in the East, and frequent newspaper communications and interviews, he did a great deal toward removing prejudices and adding to the good reputation of New Mexico. On the 2nd of April, 1889, he was appointed governor of the Territory by President Harrison, and was inaugurated in front of the capital on April 17. The demonstration on this occasion was by far the largest ever known in New Mexico, a great procession escorting him from the depot and about 5000 persons being present at the ceremony.

Governor Prince is indeed a man of whom the Territory may well be proud and of whom it may be said, "His aims are noble and his methods just." He has been a leader in public thought, an authority in law and legislation, and there are few instances where a single mind has impressed itself so strongly upon the affairs of the people as his. He is a man of great and simple nature, of high intellectual powers, of sober and solid judgment, and he has brought to the executive office a well trained mind and a keenness of perception in financial matters that qualify him to make a successful and popular executive.

IV

In Memory of
L. BRADFORD PRINCE
President of the Society
Historical Society of New Mexico, No. 25, April 23, 1923

Address by Frank W. Clancy

Ladies and Gentlemen:

Although it has been some months since the painful event occurred, this is the first opportunity when announcement could be made to our society of the loss which it has sustained in the death of our president, L. Bradford Prince, who for nearly 40 years was the sustaining influence and the soul of the Historical Society of New Mexico. That this has not been sooner made an occasion of commemoration by us of so great a man, is to be attributed to the fact that our loss has had such an absolutely paralyzing effect upon our activities not only as a society, but as individuals, that it has not been possible at any earlier moment to give expression to our feelings of the loss which our society has sustained, and as well the commonwealth of New Mexico at large, but some record of those feelings must be made by the society to which he so long devoted his great talents, energy and ability, after he cast his lot with the people of New Mexico.

It seems to devolve upon me, as vice-president of our society, and as a close and intimate friend of our late president for many years, to attempt to present to you and to the public, some appropriate recognition of his great character and record as a man, a publicist, a jurist, and especially as the steadfast friend through all his lifetime after he came to New Mexico, of our people with whom he made his home and with whom he identified himself in every possible honorable and unselfish way. I feel that I can not do justice to the subject, but I can not avoid responding to what seems to be a call of duty, from the varying standpoints of public citizenship and personal friendship.

To attempt here to make anything like a record of his career and varied achievements is simply impossible. For me to make a mere enumeration of all that he did, of all that he accomplished in public office, of all that he gave to the public in the way of literary authorship, and of what he gave of himself in many ways to the general welfare, would make a book of hundreds of pages, and would be inappropriate here and would exhaust your patience.

He was born in Flushing, Long Island, in June, 1840 and died at the same place, which had been the home of the Prince family for generations, December 8, 1922, so that he was in his 83rd year at the time of his death, and his public activities which began while he was still a boy, continued until the year of his death. He organized political committees before he was 21 years of age, and while, as before stated, it is useless to attempt even a mere enumeration of all that he accomplished, yet mention must be made of a few things.

He wrote, before he graduated from the law school of Columbia university, a book of 125 pages, which was published by G. P. Putnam & Son in 1867, entitled, *E Pluribus Unum*, or "American Nationality," and was both historical and political in the proper sense of that word, and reviewed our early attempts at government, beginning with colonial times down to and through the chaotic period of the Articles of Confederation, which led to the formation of our Constitution, expounded that Constitution, and told of our great growth and prosperity thereunder, all in a most wonderful and masterly manner, so that it might well be reproduced in whole or in part, with great benefit at the present time, when attacks are made upon our time-honored Constitution by so many different kinds of honest but misguided minds, from the anarchist and socialist, who sees nothing but evil in all existing forms of government and would destroy them by violence if necessary, and they say it is necessary, to those who call themselves merely progressive and would change and destroy by piecemeal here and there, apparently unconscious of the destructive nature of their efforts. This little book received unstinted praise from many of the men of that day, such as Henry Wilson, Zach Chandler, Millard Fillmore, Reuben E. Fenton, Schuyler Colfax, George William Curtis and even Roscoe Conkling, although later he became personally hostile to Mr. Prince, and was perhaps the principal cause of his leaving New York to come to New Mexico.

His public career in the political arena began in 1871, when he was elected, and later again and again re-elected, as a Republican from a strongly Democratic district to the legislature of the state of New York, where he served with distinction, especially in connection with securing needed amendments to the constitution of the state in 1874, and the impeachment of dishonest judges of the worst period of official corruption in the state.

If he had remained in New York, there is no flight of imagination which can reach the possibilities—the probabilities—of what he might have attained in national politics. Even after he came to New Mexico, again and again he was urged by his former associates to return to New York, with the certainty, as they believed, that he could go to congress as a representative or even as a senator, from the Empire state; but he early became so fascinated and even infatuated with New Mexico and its people, that he turned a deaf ear to all such urgings.

In the '70s of the 19th century, Roscoe Conkling was the dominant political power in New York, and while in some ways he was a great man, of varied talents, he demanded from his party abject and servile obedience, was petulant and childishly vindictive towards all who would not bow the knee to Conkling, and Mr. Prince was not one of that kind, so that when opportunity presented itself for him to get away from New York, it seemed then the part of wisdom to embrace that opportunity. The dominance and downfall of Conkling, due to the qualities above mentioned, are a part of the political history of our country, and need not be considered now.

In 1878 the president offered to appoint Mr. Prince

governor of the territory of Idaho, but he conceived a prejudice against Idaho, after calling upon the delegate from that territory, and finding him without shoes and with his wool-clad feet obtrusively elevated to a highly unornamental position, and declined the appointment. This was not perhaps altogether reasonable, as that delegate may not have been a fair representative of the people of his territory. Shortly thereafter the president appointed him chief justice of New Mexico, and he arrived in Santa Fe in the winter of 1878-79. From that time on he was a prominent and active part of New Mexico, giving his time and great abilities to everything which could tend to the development of his adopted land.

As a judge, with six counties over the district courts of which he presided, there had not been, nor has there been since, anyone in such a position in New Mexico who disposed of so much business in the same length of time. My personal acquaintance with him began in 1879. I became clerk of his court in the summer of that year, and so continued until he resigned in 1882, and thereafter until March, 1883.

His only fault as a judge, if it were a fault, was in the excessive amount of work which he performed and imposed upon the members of the bar and court officers. He was never harsh or inconsiderate of litigants or their lawyers. I remember having seen, more than once in the district court in the old town of Las Vegas, when counsel asked for time to get a witness or client from the other side of the Gallinas, that he would grant the request, but in order to expedite business, he would empanel another jury for the trial of a different case and proceed therewith until the absentee arrived, when the trial of the first case would be resumed.

At that term in Las Vegas he opened court at 8 in the morning, adjourned from 12 to 1 to permit the eating of a midday meal, and from 6 to 7 for supper, and never stopped before 11 at night. He was always alert, and apparently untired, but everyone else was worn out.

My personal belief is that no judge should hold court much beyond five hours in a day, as with long hours, the bench, the bar and jury are not fit to do their best work, and therefore I do not wholly approve of Judge Prince's judicial record; but it was characteristic of the man to do so much work in a limited time and do it so well. It is difficult to understand how any man could do so much of a high order of merit as he did. An instance of this is to be found in what he did quite soon after he became chief justice.

There had been a compilation of the statutes of New Mexico in 1865, which, although poorly done and badly arranged, was the book of reference of all statutes in existence in 1865, but after that there had been many sessions of the legislature, at each of which numerous statutes were enacted, and in 1879 and 1880 it was very difficult to procure a copy of the compiled laws of 1865, and almost impossible to secure a complete set of the session laws adopted after 1865. And yet Judge Prince, within a year and a half after he became judge, prepared and had published a compilation of all laws then in force, and that book was the only standard as to our statutes for the guidance of territorial and county officers, of the courts and of all the bar until some time in 1885, when the compilation of 1884 became available. I never heard of any complaint of the completeness or accuracy of Prince's compilation, and no one could understand how he found the time to do such work. A story was circulated that he did it all on the train between Santa Fe and New York, whither he went when the courts were not in session. At that time it took 48 hours—often more—to go from Santa Fe to Kansas City, and nearly as much more from there to New York. When we reflect upon the rapidity and accuracy with which that work was done, we may be able to understand, or if not to understand, to believe that he did so much work that most of men would have required a lifetime of continuous labor to accomplish. Among other things, he found time to write a history of New Mexico which is a standard work and constantly referred to by all writers on New Mexico history, and a little later the *Student's History of New Mexico*, which might be well adopted as a part of the curriculum of all schools in the state, and which ought, at least, to be in the library of every educational institution, including all high schools.

He wrote a book of nearly 400 pages on the *Spanish Mission Churches of New Mexico*, which is a treasure-house of information on a subject to which no other before him had given more than slight attention. He wrote interesting and erudite monographs on "The Stone Lions of Cochiti," and "Old Fort Marcy," and a historical review of *The Struggle for Statehood 1850 to 1910*, and a bewildering number of magazine articles and letters to the press on New Mexican subjects, which required an enormous amount of time, research and labor, difficult of belief when we consider the immense amount of time which he gave to so many other fields of work, such as the Trans-Mississippi congress, of which he was president in 1892, 1893, and 1899, the International Mining congress, of which he was vice-president in 1900-03, and in every thing connected with the Protestant Episcopal church, of which he was an untiring and devoted member, whether in national or local affairs. As I have already said, it seems an unnecessary and difficult task to attempt to enumerate the many things which he did, and all so wonderfully well.

It is much better to turn our attention to his individual characteristics as a man, in contact with his fellow beings, which so greatly endeared him to all who knew him.

First, I invite you to consider that from the very beginning of his life in New Mexico, he never failed when opportunity offered to raise his voice, or use his pen, in defense of our people of Spanish descent, against the unjust and villainous attacks upon them made by English-speaking persons inspired by ignorance and ignoble race prejudice, against a kindly, hospitable, open-hearted people, who have from 1846 received and treated the gringos who came here as their conquerors and oppressors with a degree of forbearance and toleration which is almost incredible. He thoroughly appreciated their good traits and, with that sense of justice which was always a part of his nature, he was ever ready in every possible way to give expression to his feelings in their behalf. This is only one evidence of his just and kindly nature, which was readily aroused by any exhibition of dishonesty and unfairness, whether in the form of the disgraceful neglect by our national government to keep its promises, of which a most glaring instance can be found in the failure to pay what are known as the French Spoliation Claims, as to which he made a violent and memorable attack and protest, or in the form of intolerance, political, religious or racial.

This naturally leads one to the consideration of his toleration of every form of honest opinion, no matter how divergent from his own. He was one of the most devoted and zealous members of the Episcopal church in the United States, taking an active and leading part in all concerns of that church, national or local, from early youth to the end of his life, yet he was never known to say an unkindly word, nor can anyone who knew him believe that he ever harbored even an unkindly thought as to any other form of honest religious belief.

He was a total abstainer from alcoholic or even vinous liquors, but he never said a word or had a thought of criticism of those whose habits of life were different from his own. He never sought to impose upon any fellow being his own standard or conduct as that to which others must conform, whether by moral suasion or by legislative mandate.

He was a Republican in politics from conviction based upon fundamental principles of political thought, but he was never harsh or unfair to his adversaries, and as to this I feel moved to become reminiscent. He believed in party politics and party organization as the safeguard of our institutions and form of government. In 1882, while he was judge, prompted by his years of success in politics in New York, he conceived the idea that he might reasonably hope to get the nomination for delegate to congress in that year, but believing that there would be gross impropriety in seeking other and political office while occupying a judicial position, an idea which has since been embodied to some extent in our state constitution, which declares that no judge shall be nominated or elected to any other than a judicial office, he resigned his office as judge with the avowed purpose of seeking the nomination for delegate to congress.

The convention to make the nomination was held in the new town of Albuquerque, which was then in its beginning, and he was defeated by what his supporters believed to be unfair and dishonest tactics of the opposition. After the nomination was made, there was an assembly of his disappointed and angry supporters in an unfinished storeroom, somewhere north of Railroad avenue, and there were many loud and vociferous appeals to him to run as an independent candidate, but after listening until the angry ones had somewhat talked themselves out, he addressed them something like this, for I cannot recall his exact language, "No, gentlemen, I cannot do that; I am a Republican and believe in party organization, and to preserve that organization is of more importance than the gratification of any man's individual ambition. I cannot be an independent candidate." His calm words quieted the angry excitement and the junta soon dispersed.

Two years later he was the regular nominee of the Republican convention, but a defeated candidate from the southern end of New Mexico, who had not had the political party education or training which New York had given Judge Prince, but looked on a political contest as one of purely personal character, with his friends bolted and made a campaign as an independent candidate without any reasonable hope of success, and thereby defeated Judge Prince, who lost by a plurality of about a thousand only, and thereafter until 1894, New Mexico was steadily represented in Congress by a Democrat. In the campaign of 1884 he was doubtful of success, but declared that, having been selected by the convention as its candidate, it was his duty as a Republican to make the best fight possible, even if he were certain to be defeated. He would have been elected if some disaffected members of the party had not been lukewarm in their support.

He was appointed governor of the territory of New Mexico in 1889, and served in that position for four years, until the national administration passed over to the Democratic party. Of his administration as governor, it is sufficient to say that it was creditable to him and of benefit to New Mexico. It will be recalled that during that period, in 1891, the public school system much as it exists today, was created by legislative action, largely due to his influence as our chief executive. Animated by a regard for the historic past, and by what seemed to him to be the natural fitness of things, he made his residence while governor in this Old Palace of the Governors under Spanish, Mexican and American governments, where we now stand, and, with the assistance of his brilliantly gifted wife, made it the scene of social functions of the most varied and ornate character.

This naturally leads me to say a word about his wife, who survives him, Mary Catharine Beardsley, daughter of a distinguished officer in the Union army during the great Civil War, of Oswego, New York, connected with many of the prominent families of that historic region of north central New York, as to her must be given the principal credit of the brilliant social success of her husband's administration as governor.

One of the most important and enduring achievements of Governor Prince was the creation by him in 1909, of the Spanish-American Normal School, which is located at El Rito. I am told that this school has been of great and most beneficial importance to the development of our educational facilities. For several years after this school was established he was president of its governing board, and many of his friends felt grieved and aggrieved that he was not restored to that board by the governor under the last Republican administration, in 1921, and were inclined to consider that the failure so to restore him was a sin of omission of that administration, as that school which he had created was very dear to his heart, and he was then still in perfect mental vigor, as indeed he remained up to the time of his death, and with sufficient physical strength to discharge the duties of the position with benefit to the public interest.

Coming now to the subject of our own society, it may truthfully be said that of all his varied interests and activities in many fields, only a few of which have been touched upon in what I have set forth, there was nothing which became so thoroughly a part of his life, and so engrossed and permeated his mind and almost every thought, as did this society and all matters connected with it.

The Historical Society of New Mexico was created by a special act of the legislative assembly of New Mexico on February 2, 1860, which was not long before the Civil War. What were its activities immediately after its creation, I do not know, but it is certain that during the war, and for years thereafter, it remained in a state of suspended animation until about 1880, when through the efforts of Governor Ritch, a man of high character with imagination and ideals for the future, the society was reorganized with Ritch as president. Right here, if time and your patience would permit, I would like to expatiate at length upon the great value of imagination, which is not, by the generality of people, even yet thoroughly appreciated, but without which nothing great has ever been accomplished in art, science, literature, philosophy, religion or government, but being of a kind and benevolent disposition, I forbear.

Governor Ritch at that time was able to do nothing more than to lay some foundation for the future, but in 1883 Governor Prince became our president, a man who combined imagination with practical executive ability, and he soon infused life into us. He gave his time, varied research, and even his private means to the acquisition of objects of historical interest. Almost everything in our present collections, is due to his personal exertions, whether it be from Indian, Mexican, Spanish or American sources. We may well feel some pride in what has been accomplished, but we should not forget that but little is due to our individual efforts, or to our collective efforts as a society, and that nearly all is due to our late president, L. Bradford Prince, after he took charge of our interests and put some life into us, beginning the arduous work of collecting objects of historic interest from all available sources, the work of arranging these acquisitions in presentable shape being in itself a task of great difficulty. In this part of the work he had the valuable assistance of Mrs. Prince, as much interested as he, who arranged, classified and labeled with her own hands the greatly diversified objects, and arranged them appropriately in cases and shelves, many of which were the creations of her own zealous and skillful hands.

In grateful remembrance of that great man and his exertions, we should strive to preserve, as he always sought, the identity of this society and its collections, and I call upon all of you to join in efforts to accomplish that purpose, first of which should be some intelligent effort toward increasing our membership.

Before closing I feel impelled to recur to what I earlier referred to, and that is the personality of our departed and beloved president. He was of most distinguished ancestry, as far as ancestry can go in our comparatively young country, as may be apparent from the fact that he was a member of such societies as the Sons of the Revolution, the Order of the Cincinnati, the Mayflower Descendants of the Colonial Wars, and of the War of 1812.

He was a direct lineal descendant of William Bradford, who came over in the Mayflower in 1620, and was governor of the Plymouth colony from the spring of 1621 until shortly before his death in 1657, with the exception of five years, 1633, 1634, 1636, 1638, and 1644.

The Encyclopaedia Britannica says of him:

"Bradford's rule was firm and judicious, and to his guidance more than that of any other man the prosperity of the Plymouth colony was due. His tact and kindness in dealing with the Indians helped to relieve the colony from conflicts with which almost every other settlement was afflicted."

To those who believe in the influence of heredity, there must seem to be found in L. Bradford Prince a survival of the traits and temperament of William Bradford. He had the "tact and kindness" in dealing with all kinds of men which William Bradford had "in dealing with the Indians." He was most human and humane in all relations of life, and in Shakespearean language, you may all well join me in saying,

"He was a man, take him for all in all, I shall not look upon his like again."

Resolutions of the Board of Regents of the State Museum

WHEREAS, in due course of nature, and ripe in years and honors the earthly life of Honorable L. Bradford Prince, President of the Historical Society of New Mexico, ended December 8, 1922, thus forever stilling the compelling call of duty, and the urge of helpful service to his fellows. Like autumn fruit, he lingered long and it was even wondered at that he dropped no sooner. Nature seemed to have wound him up for four score years, yet ran he freely on three winters more; until, like a clock worn out with eating Time, the wheels of weary life at last stood still.

Born in Flushing, New York, July 3, 1840, of a long line of illustrious, one hundred per cent American ancestors, he measured up completely to their standards of citizenship, during his many years of active life and service to his fellow-citizens, in his native state of New York, his adopted state of New Mexico, and to the Republic at large. Early in life he developed an aptitude for political matters. By persistent, toilsome effort, he stored his splendid intellect with valuable knowledge. He graduated from the Columbia Law School.

While still a young man, he became interested in politics. He was a delegate to all the state conventions in New York, from 1866 to 1878, and was elected a delegate to the National Republican convention which nominated General Grant for President. The following year he became a member of the New York State Republican Committee. In 1870, '71, '72, '73 and '74, he was a member of the New York Assembly, and in 1875, was elected to the State Senate by an overwhelming majority. His public service there was highly honorable and splendidly useful.

Coming to New Mexico in the later seventies, he immediately took great interest in this, then territory, and soon came to the front as one of the most influential advocates of statehood. In 1878, he was appointed Chief Justice of the Supreme Court of New Mexico, by President Rutherford B. Hayes. He served in that capacity until May, 1882, when he resigned. The efficiency and impartiality of his administration as Chief Justice were approved by the business interests of the territory. He showed a remarkable capacity for expediting business that came before the Court.

"And he judged therein as a just man should; His words were wise and his rule was good."

There was no time after he became a citizen of New Mexico that he was not foremost in the ranks of our citizens, doing his utmost, at home and abroad, for the welfare and prosperity of the people. He framed the act under which the Bureau of Immigration was organized. As early as 1881, he prepared a compilation of the laws of New Mexico. In 1883, he became President of the Historical Society of New Mexico. For years he was identified, either as officer or member, with the Trans-Mississippi and National Irrigation Congresses, where he accomplished much for the best interests of the entire west.

In the spring of 1889, President Benjamin Harrison appointed Honorable L. Bradford Prince governor of New Mexico. His administration of the affairs of the territory, while governor, was characterized by its progressive spirit, always having in view the educational, social and industrial advancement of the territory. Socially, no occupant of the old Palace of the Governors, before or since, so elaborately entertained the people of all classes. His wife, Mrs. Mary C. Prince, nee Beardsley, of Oswego, New York, a descendant of one of the most prominent families of that state, was a charming hostess, and a great favorite with the guests on these occasions.

After retiring from the office of governor, Governor Prince practiced his profession in the courts of New Mexico, devoting considerable time to horticultural pursuits, maintaining his legal residence in Rio Arriba County, near Chamita. From this county he became a member of the legislative council, in the 38th legislative assembly.

But now his work is finished. He has gone to a well earned rest. His reward is to be that of the faithful. We shall miss him.

But his good works will live as long as enlightened citizenship stands ready to offer up the supreme sacrifice, on the altar of freedom. The key to his life was service. His philosophy of life was helpfulness. He accepted the fundamental truth that he who serves best is greatest among us, and he who serves well shall indeed be well served in his own soul.

He felt that representative government comes to an end when outside influence of any kind is substituted for the judgment of the representative. He deplored the unsound social and economical theories that deluge our country from time to time, and felt that they are not the progeny of stalwart men and women; that sound bodies do not breed unsound doctrine. That along with a vigorous physical training, should go a mental calisthenics for creating healthful thoughts, and that after all, it must be remembered that "as a man thinketh in his heart, so is he."

He held that government is not-must not be-a cold, impersonal machine, but a real, genuine, human agency, appealing to reason, satisfying the heart, full of mercy, assisting the good, resisting the wrong, delivering the weak from any imposition of the strong. That this is not paternalism, is not servitude imposed from without, but freedom of a righteous, self-direction from within. That laws are not manufactured, are not imposed; but are rules of action, based upon the principles of eternal Truth; and that there is no greater service this Republic can render the oppressed of the earth than to maintain inviolate the freedom of its own citizens.

He had complete faith in the moral power of the United States. He believed that the nation with the greatest moral power will win; that this power gave us independence under Washington and freedom under Lincoln. That here, in the United States, right has never lost, and wrong has never won. However powerful the forces of evil may appear, there are somewhere, more powerful forces of righteousness. That we have a priceless heritage of confidence and courage, and that justice is our might. With our late lamented President Harding, he proclaimed Americanism and acclaimed America, in the Spirit of the Republic.

Like other great Americans, he thanked God that the spirit of a free people can be created, animated and cheered out of the storehouse of its historic recollections. He thanked God that the exemplars of patriotic virtue have abounded in our own country, on our own soil; that strains of the noblest sentiment that ever swelled in the breast of man are breathing to us out of every page of our country's history in the native eloquence of our native tongue; that the Colonial and Provincial Councils of America exhibit to us models of the spirit and character which gave Greece and Rome their name and their praise among nations.

His interpretation of patriotism included more than a willingness and readiness to fight and die for one's country and its institutions. He believed that if a man loves his country and is true to her institutions, and is affectionately concerned for their quality and permanence, there will be something which he will be all the time doing in her behalf. To his way of thinking, going to war is only a small and incidental part of the matter. He felt that what our country needs most is men who will *live* for her, and during all of her times of peace, work for the consummation of her noble ideals.

He believed that the spirit of nationalism is essential to the perpetuity of this Republic. That such a spirit is as the sun in the heavens, diffusing light and warmth, and by its subtle influence holding the planets in their orbits and preserving the harmony of the universe. So he maintained that the sentiment of nationality in a people diffuses life and protection in every direction, holding the faces of Americans always toward their homes, and preserving the harmony of all. He cherished the idea that while the states have their rights, sacred and inviolable, which we should guard with untiring vigilance, never permitting an encroachment upon them, and ever remembering that such encroachment is as much a violation of the Constitution of the United States as to encroach upon the rights of the general government, still we should ever bear in mind that the states are but subordinate parts of one great nation, that the nation is over all, even as God is over the universe.

Longfellow had Governor Prince's type in mind when he wrote:

> "The heights by great men reached and kept
> Were not attained by sudden flight,
> But they, while their companions slept,
> Were toiling upward in the night."

THEREFORE, Be it Resolved, that in the death of Honorable L. Bradford Prince, New Mexico has sustained an irreparable loss; that Santa Fe has lost one of its most illustrious, useful and patriotic citizens, and that the great republic of the United States is vastly poorer because of his passing.

Resolved, That the Board of Regents of the State Museum extend to his bereaved wife and family its sincere and heartfelt sympathy, in this day of their affliction, and,

Resolved, That these resolutions be spread upon the records of the Board of Regents of the State Museum of New Mexico, and that a copy be presented to the widow of the late Honorable L. Bradford Prince.

RALPH E. TWITCHELL,
Chairman
FRANK SPRINGER
JNO. R. McFIE
N. B. LAUGHLIN
J. L. SELIGMAN,
Committee.

V

FACSIMILE OF 1910 EDITION

NEW MEXICO'S

STRUGGLE FOR STATEHOOD

Sixty Years of Effort to Obtain
Self Government.

BY
L. BRADFORD PRINCE,
President Historical Society of New Mexico,
Ex-Assemblyman and Senator, New York,
Ex-Chief Justice and Governor, New Mexico.

FIRST EDITION.

SANTA FE, N. M.
THE NEW MEXICAN PRINTING COMPANY
1910

Act of 1910.—The Historic Pens.

TABLE OF CONTENTS.

CHAPTER I.   Page
    The Beginning of the Struggle.............. 5
CHAPTER II.
    Convention of 1848........................ 9
CHAPTER III.
    Convention of 1849........................ 13
CHAPTER IV.
    The Constitution of 1850 and First State Government........................ 17
CHAPTER V.
    Legislative Effort and Constitution of 1872... 24
CHAPTER VI.
    Congressional Action to 1876............... 34
CHAPTER VII.
    Congressional Action 1876 to 1895.......... 37
CHAPTER VIII.
    Constitution of 1890...................... 48
CHAPTER IX.
    Proposed Changes of Name................ 60
CHAPTER X.
    Favorable Influences...................... 65
CHAPTER XI.
    National Conventions..................... 70
CHAPTER XII.
    Hearings in Washington................... 74
CHAPTER XIII.
    Statements to Committees................. 81

TABLE OF CONTENTS.

CHAPTER XIV. Page
    Congressional 1895 to 1901.................. 91
CHAPTER XV.
    The Beveridge Committee............ 95
CHAPTER XVI.
    The Right to Self Government............... 102
CHAPTER XVII.
    Joint Statehood Movement of 1906.... ... 107
CHAPTER XVIII.
    Proposed Convention of 1907............... 113
CHAPTER XIX
    Congressional Action, 1901 to 1910.......... 118
CHAPTER XX.
    Final Success. 124

INTRODUCTION.

Self-government is the fundamental principle of a Republic; pre-eminently of the American Republic.

It is the keynote of the Declaration of Independence, and the foundation of the Constitution.

"Governments derive their just powers from the consent of the governed."

"We, the people of the United States....do ordain and establish this Constitution."

Yet, in New Mexico, American citizens have been deprived of self-government for over sixty years; and that, against their repeated remonstrances; and for at least a quarter of a century without a vestige of right or reason.

Now, when this strange anomaly is about to disappear, and this long period of un-American bondage to end, it seems proper to review the history of those years, and of the Struggle for Statehood which has continued through their whole duration.

Again, there are few who appreciate the remarkable record which New Mexico has achieved as a constitution-maker. No Territory ever framed so many constitutions; no Territory ever framed them so well.

The three that are in print, those of 1850, 1872 and 1890, are all models of excellence, instruments of which any people may be proud.

It seems well, just as the final constitution is to be formulated, that the excellences of these should be realized and perhaps in some respects followed.

That of 1850, especially, is a marvel. When we remember that it was written less than four years after the American occupation; by a convention, over nine-tenths of whose membership was of Spanish descent and very brief experience in the American governmental system, it is not simply creditable, it is almost a miracle of excellence; and its courageous declaration as to human slavery,

INTRODUCTION.

under the peculiar circumtances, and in view of the sacrifice which it involved, is beyond all praise.

There is another reason which seems to render such a retrospect timely. Perhaps nowhere in history is there such a series of failures, in what at the time seemed almost certainty, through unlooked for and often insignificant causes.

Statehood was almost attained in 1850; it was lost by a handshake in 1875, by a sudden impetuous word in 1889, by a shiver of malaria and a miscalculation of time in 1894.

At least a dozen times the passage of an Enabling Act has been considered certain, and its failure has come from some unimportant cause. Today, the fruition of long effort, the victorious end of the protracted struggle, seems at hand. But this retrospect may teach the value of extreme care and tactful consideration, that the chalice may not again be dashed from the thirsty lips, and American citizens be longer consigned to political bondage.

Struggle for Statehood

CHAPTER I.

THE BEGINNING OF THE STRUGGLE.

In no part of the United States has there ever been such a protracted struggle for self-government as in New Mexico. In no other case has Statehood been so long withheld.

The inhabited parts of the Louisiana Purchase, in the vicinity of New Orleans and St. Louis, acquired in 1803, were admitted as the State of Louisiana in 1812 and that of Missouri in 1821. Florida, which was acquired from Spain in 1821, became a State in 1845. Of the territory ceded by Mexico in 1848, California, which was then the only inhabited portion except New Mexico, was admitted in 1850. The vast domain north and south of the Ohio, roamed over by Indians at the foundation of the national government, was divided into self-governing States as fast as white settlement permitted; Ohio, Indiana and Illinois becoming States in 1802, 1816 and 1818; and Mississippi and Alabama in 1817 and 1819.

New Mexico was acquired with California and the remainder of northern Mexico by occupation in 1846 and cession in 1848, and yet more than sixty years afterwards it was still struggling to obtain the fundamental right of a free people and still meeting opposition and defeat.

The struggle for Statehood began almost as soon as the American occupation. In the speeches and proclamations of Gov. Kearny language was used which aroused hope, if it did not give promise, of self-government. In the first address in front of the Palace, on August 19th, 1846, he announced the intention to "establish a civil government on a republican basis similar to those of our own States."

In the formal proclamation of annexation issued three days later, appeared these words: "It is the wish and intention of the United States to provide for New Mexico a free government, with the least possible delay, similar to those in the United States."

By Article IX of the Treaty of Guadalupe Hidalgo it is provided that the people of the Territory annexed to the United States "shall be incorporated into the Union of the United States and be admitted at the proper time (to be judged of by the Congress of the United States) to the enjoyment of all the rights of citizens of the United States according to the principles of the Constitution."

The ratifications of the Treaty were exchanged at Queretero, May 30, 1848, and it was formally proclaimed at Washington on July 4, 1848, and at Santa Fe in August of that year.

By this re-establishment of peace the military rule in the newly acquired territory, together with the civil governments which had been set up by military authority in California and New Mexico, legally ceased to exist, but the practical conditions required some regular government to act until Congress should provide for the future; and the national administration took the ground that "the termination of the war left an existing government, a government de facto, in full operation; and this will continue, with the presumed consent of the people, until Congress shall provide for them a Territorial government." The advice of the President was that the people should "live peaceably and quietly under the existing government for a few months" until Congress could act deliberately and wisely.

Hon. Thomas H. Benton, then in the height of his influence and power as Senator from Missouri, was greatly interested in the condition of the new domain, and especially of New Mexico; and in default of any representation of the acquired territory, in Congress, he cheerfully assumed the place of its protector and was looked up to by the body of the people as their best friend and their political guide. The view that he took of the situation was that no congressional enabling act or other action by Congress was necessary, but that the people as American citizens had the right to frame and adopt a constitution, organize their local government, and then ask Congress to admit them into the Union and afford to them proper representation in both Houses of the national legislature. Under date of August 28th, 1848, he addressed an open letter to the people of California and New Mexico, in which he advised them "to meet in convention, provide for a cheap and simple government, and take care of yourselves until Congress can provide for you."

Meanwhile, under the provisions of the Kearny Code, the first legislature of New Mexico had been elected, and had held its regular session, beginning on December 6th, 1847. The Council consisted of seven members elected by districts, with Antonio Sandoval of Bernalillo County as President; and the House of twenty-one members with W. Z. Angney as Speaker.

This legislature could do little but local business, as the Treaty of Peace with Mexico was not yet signed, but it has been rendered famous by the bold and excellent character of the Message delivered to the joint session by Gov. Donaciano Vigil, especially relative to public education. After lamenting that there was but one public school in the Territory, and that the funds were only sufficient for one teacher, he says: "It is evident that the means of obtaining an education are exceedingly limited and that the facilities should be greatly increased, that opportunities for learning should be given to all, to the poor as well as the rich, and if possible a school placed in every town and neighborhood of the Territory. If our government here is to be republican, if it is to be based upon democratic principles, and if the will of the majority is one day to be law of the land and the government of the people, it is most important for this will to be properly exercised. The people must be enlightened and instructed so that every man shall be able to read and inform himself of matters important to his country and his government. It is true that the available means which could be applied at present to the cause of education are small. But for the promotion of so desirable an object they should be both increased and economized. All that the legislature can do for the cause of education of the people is most earnestly pressed upon them, and to this object I give my hearty approval and co-operation."

Thus the first official utterance in New Mexican legislative halls was for education and progress.

CHAPTER II.

CONVENTION OF 1848.

The advice of Senator Benton was quickly followed. New Mexico was without any legal government since the Treaty of Guadalupe Hidalgo had ended the regime of military occupation, and the continuance of the de facto military authority was but a temporary make-shift justifiable by the peculiar conditions. The people were anxious for almost any form of government which would be regular in form and civil in character.

Under call from Gov. Vigil, a Convention was held at Santa Fe on Oct. 10th, 1848, and organized by the election of Antonio Jose Martinez of Taos (the celebrated Padre Martinez) as President, J. M. Giddings as Clerk, Henry Henrie as Interpreter, and Thomas White as doorkeeper. Gov. Vigil took an active part in the proceedings, although, perhaps from a strict regard for the proprieties of his position, he did not sign the Petition to Congress.

Francisco Sarracino, who had been Governor of New Mexico under the Mexican regime, in 1834, Governor Vigil, James Quinn and Juan Perea were appointed a committee to draft a memorial to Congress expressing the views of the Convention. They reported a form of Petition, which was unanimously adopted, which looked to the immediate establishment of a Territorial Government, entirely civil in its character, which then appeared the most feasible method of obtaining relief from military rule and some regular legal system, by act of Congress. This Petition contained the following paragraphs, together with others of less importance:

"We, the people of New Mexico, respectfully petition Congress for the speedy organization of a territorial civil government.

"We respectfully petition Congress to establish a government purely civil in its character.

"We respectfully, but firmly, protest against the dismemberment of our territory in favor of Texas or from any cause.

"We do not desire to have domestic slavery within our borders; and until the time shall arrive for admission into the Union of States, we desire to be protected by Congress against the introduction of slaves into the Territory.

"We desire a local legislature, such as is prescribed by the laws of New Mexcio, September 22, 1846, subject to the usual veto of Congress.

"We desire that our interests be represented by a delegate admitted to a seat in Congress."

This was dated October 14th, 1848, and was signed by the following members of the convention:

ANTONIO J. MARTINES,
ELIAS P. WEST,
JUAN PEREA,
FRANCISCO SARRACINO,
GREGORIO VIGIL,
RAMON LUNA,
ANTONIO SAIS,
SANTIAGO ARCHULETA,
JAMES QUINN,
MANUEL A. OTERO,
CHARLES BEAUBIEN,
JOSE PLEY.

On motion of Gov. Vigil, it was determined to send copies to Senator Benton of Missouri and Senator Clayton of Delaware, with the request that they represent the interests of New Mexico in the Senate until it should have regularly represented members.

It is recorded in Niles' Register, Vol. 74, p. 407, that when this petition was received and read in the Senate on Dec. 13th, it caused quite a storm of comment, especially from the pro-slavery senators, who were astounded at what they termed "the insolence" of the language of the document.

Nothing resulted from the action of this convention, and the people continued to be very restless under the irregular authority of the military commanders. They were divided into two parties, one anxious for Statehood, and the other believing that a regular territorial organization was all that could be obtained and that therefore their efforts should be bent in that direction.

But in fact the wishes of the people of New Mexico were considered in Washington then but little more than in more modern days, and the Territory was only a pawn in the game of national politics and in the mighty conflict between the slave power and the aroused sentiment in favor of freedom.

The South had brought about the annexation of Texas, and followed it up by the war against Mexico, in order to acquire a vast additional area south of Mason and Dixon's line supposed to be suited to slave labor and expected to be cut up into future slave states. But there was disappointment as to the anticipated results. The discovery of gold in California had led to a phenomenal emigration to the Pacific, largely from the North and opposed to slavery. The rapid increase of population there made it almost impossible to refuse Statehood to the Golden State, and the only way to keep even a balance between the sections was to form a slave State in New Mexico. But to the surprise of the southern leaders, it was found that the Mexican population was unalterably opposed to slavery. In the very first New Mexican convention, as we have just seen, they spoke on that subject in no uncertain tones.

The situation was further complicated by the claim of Texas to the ownership of all the Territory east of the Rio Grande, which was vigorously maintained by the Lone Star State. Though without any foundation in law or history, and absurd in view of the fact that for two hundred and fifty years New Mexico had existed as it does today, on both sides of the River and with its capital and chief towns on the east side, and that its authorities through all that period had exercised undisputed authority over the country east of the Rio Grande, as far as the European settlements extended, and on the buffalo plains as far as the western line of the great domain then known as Louisiana, yet the United States, by assuming in the

Mexican War that Texas rightfully included the country between the Nueces and the Rio Grande, had given its claim a kind of endorsement which now was a source of much embarrassment and of most animated debates in Congress. Thus the fate of New Mexico depended far more on the strength of sectional divisions and the exigencies of party policies in Washington, than on the acts and wishes of its own people.

CHAPTER III.

CONVENTION OF 1849.

Still these people were unceasing in their struggles to obtain some regular form of government under which their rights should be protected.

In deference to this sentiment, in the summer of 1849, Lieut. Col. Beall, acting as Governor during the absence of Col. Washington, issued a proclamation for the election of Delegates to a Convention to consider a plan for the civil government of New Mexico. This convention consisted of nineteen Delegates, apportioned among the seven counties into which the Territory was then divided; and it met at Santa Fe on the 24th of September. The Journal of this interesting body has recently been re-printed by the Historical Society of New Mexico, as its publication No. 10, from the original document presented in Congress, Feb. 25, 1850, and printed as H. R. Mis. Doc. No. 39, 31st Cong. Ist. Ses.

The record is entitled as follows:

JOURNAL AND PROCEEDINGS OF A CONVENTION OF DELEGATES ELECTED

By the people of New Mexico, held at Santa Fe on the 24th of September, 1849, presenting a plan for a civil government of said Territory of New Mexico and asking the action of Congress thereon.

Convention held at the city of Santa Fe, Territory of New Mexico, composed of delegates elected by the people of the different counties, in conformity with the proclamation of Lieutenant Colonel Beall, civil and military commandant of the Territory of New Mexico, in the absence of Lieutenant Colonel J. M. Washington, civil and military governor.

The following was the membership of the Convention by Counties:

Bernalillo—Manuel Armijo y Mestas, Ambrosio Armijo y Ortiz.

Rio Arriba—Joseph Nangle, Salvador Lucero.
San Miguel—Gregorio Vigil, Manuel Antonio Baca.
Santa Ana—Miguel Montoya, Francisco Tomas Baca.
Santa Fe—Manuel Alvarez, E. Vaudry Deroin, W. Z. Angney.
Taos—Ceran St. Vrain, Antonio Jose Martin, Antonio Leroux.
Valencia—Juan Jose Sanches, William Curtis Skinner, Mariano Silva, Antonio Jose Otero, Manuel Antonio Otero.

On motion of Ceran St. Vrain, the Rev. Cura Antonio Jose Martinez was unanimously elected President; but in the subsequent election and other votes there was a uniform division of fifteen to four, the minority consisting of the three Santa Fe members, Alvarez, Deroin, and Angney, and Dr. Nangle of Rio Arriba.

The Convention elected a Delegate to represent New Mexico in the Congress of the United States, Hugh N. Smith being chosen for that position; and subsequently named ex-Governor Francisco Sarracino as "alternate delegate."

A committee of five was then appointed to report the basis of a constitution for the government of the Territory and instructions for the delegate to Congress.

On the third day of the Session, by invitation, his Excellency Gov. Washington, Hon. Joab Houghton, Justice of the Supreme Court, and Hon. Donaciano Vigil, Secretary of the Territory, appeared and were escorted by a committee to seats with the President.

The plan of government, or constitution, adopted as a recommendation to Congress, shows excellent judgment, and was largely followed in the provisions of the Organic Act of 1850. It is brief and left all details to be settled by subsequent legislation. The following provisions may be cited as showing both good sense and foresight:

"Art. II. Sec. 15. No person who now is, or hereafter may be, a collector or holder of public money, or assistant or deputy thereof, shall be eligible to any office of profit or trust, until he shall have accounted for, and paid over all moneys for which he may be acountable as such collector or holder; and no person who shall have directly or indirectly given any bribe to procure his election or appointment to any office, or who shall have been convicted of perjury or other infamous crime, shall be eligible to any office of honor, profit, or trust within this territory, or shall be allowed the right of suffrage.

"Art. III. Sec. 2. The supreme court shall consist of four judges, one to be supreme or appellate judge, and the other three to be district judges, for the hearing and adjudication of law cases, and associates of the supreme judge in all cases of appeal; and the judge who tried the case shall not be allowed to sit in the appellate court."

The instructions given to the delegates were practical, and were introduced by a preamble which sets forth in such strong terms the unfortunate situation of the people that it is worthy of reproduction. It reads as follows:

INSTRUCTIONS AS ADOPTED BY THE CONVENTION.

"We, the people of New Mexico, in convention assembled, having elected a delegate to represent this Territory in the Congress of the United States, and to urge upon the supreme government a redress of our grievances, and the protection due to us as citizens of our common country, under the constitution, instruct him as follows: That whereas, for the last three years, we have suffered under the paralyzing effects of a government undefined and doubtful in its character, inefficient to protect the rights of the people, or to discharge the high and absolute duty of every government, the enforcement and regular administration of its own laws, in consequence of which, industry and enterprise are paralyzed, and discontent and confusion prevail throughout the land; the want of proper protection against the various barbarous tribes of Indians that surround us on every side, has prevented the extension of settlements upon our valuable public domain, and rendered utterly futile every attempt to explore or develop the great resources of the territory; surrounded by the Eutaws, Comanches, and Apaches, on the north, east and south, by the Navajos on the west, with Jicarillas within our limits, and without any adequate protection against their hostile inroads; our flocks and herds are driven off by thousands, our fellow-citizens, men, women and children are murdered or carried into captivity; many of our citizens of all ages and sexes are at this moment suffering all the horrors of barbarian bondage, and it is utterly out of our power to obtain their release from a condition to which death would be preferable; the wealth of our territory is being diminished; we have neither the means nor any adopted plan by government for the education of the rising generation; in fine, with a government temporary, doubtful, uncertain, and inefficient in character and in operation, surrounded and despoiled by barbarous foes, ruin appears inevitably before us, unless speedy and effectual protection be extended to us by the Congress of the United States."

The delegate was instructed particularly, as follows, as to the form of government desired:

"That, in case a territorial government may be obtained, he shall prefer it to a state government, and shall take for his grounds the late act constituting the people of Minnesota into a territorial government, and shall insist upon provisions at least as favorable."

"But in case the obtention of a territorial government be not feasible, but that of a state government be practicable, he shall accept one, and proceed to its organization; taking for his model the present constitution of Missouri, so far as the same is applicable to our condition."

Candidatos del Pueblo

Para Gobernador
Tomas Baca

Vice Gobernador
Manuel Alvarez

Congreso General
Wm. S. Messervy

Senadores
Jose Fco Cryba
Jose N Angel
Domingo Baca

Representantes
Miguel Sena y Romero
Melario Gonsales
Jose Jesus Montotto

Ballot at First Statehood Election. 1850,

CHAPTER IV.

THE CONSTITUTION OF 1850 AND FIRST STATE GOVERNMENT.

Meanwhile the discussion of the status of the vast domain recently acquired from Mexico continued in Congress almost incessantly and with considerable bitterness, on national and political lines. There seems to be no doubt that Gen. Taylor, from the time that he became president in March, 1849, was anxious for the admission of both California and New Mexico as States, in order to settle the question of slavery which was causing increasing excitement.

In his message to Congress he frankly announced this policy. He said: "I did not hesitate to express to the people of those territories my desire that each territory should, if prepared to comply with the requirements of the Constitution of the United States, form a plan of a State Constitution and submit the same to Congress wih a prayer for admission into the Union as a State."

In the annual message of December 4, 1849, he again evinced his interest by saying: "The people of New Mexico will also, it is believed, at no very distant period, present themselves for admission."

In the spring of 1849, James S. Calhoun, afterwards the first Governor under the Organic Act, was sent to New Mexico as Indian agent, but with semi-official instructions to favor the organization of a State government. In this he was actively aided by Manuel Alvarez, Angney, Pillans, etc., while Ceran St. Vrain, Judge Houghton, Carlos Beaubien, etc., favored a territorial form of government.

That the national government expected and desired the people to take the initiative in the matter, which down to that time had been the usual method of obtaining admission to the Union, instead of awaiting an "enabling act" from Congress; and that the right of New Mexico to Statehood was generally admitted even at that early date, is obvious from the instructions of the Secretary of War (George W.

Crawford) to Lieut. Col. McCall, dated Nov. 9, 1849, when the latter was on his way to New Mexico. Their purport will be seen from the following extract:

"Since their annexation these territories in respect to their civil government have in a great measure depended on the officers of the army there in command. This condition has arisen from the omission of Congress to provide suitable governments; and in regard to the future there is reason to believe that the difficulties of the past are still to be encountered. It is not doubted that the people of New Mexico desire and want a government organized. The question readily recurs how that government can be supplied. It is therefore deemed proper that I should say that it is not believed that the people of New Mexico are required to await the movements of the Federal Government in relation to a plan of government for the regulation of their own internal concerns. The Constitution of the United States and the late Treaty with Mexico guarantee their admission into the Union of our States, subject only to the judgment of Congress. Should the people of New Mexico wish to take any steps towards this object, it will be your duty and the duty of others with whom you are associated, not to thwart but to advance their wishes. It is their right to appear before Congress and ask for admission into the Union."

Soon after his arrival, Col. McCall spread abroad the information that Congress did not favor a territorial form of government but that President Taylor was very anxious that New Mexico should immediately become a State. Letters of the same purport were also received from Delegate Smith, who remained in Washington, although he had not been admitted to a seat in Congress; receiving 86 votes against 92, on the final action.

The result was that all parties united in the desire for a Constitutional Convention, and an important meeting was held in Santa Fe on April the 20th, 1850, where resolutions to that effect were adopted, and Col. Monroe, then Military Governor, was requested to issue a proclamation calling for an election of delegates.

This he did in April, 1850, and a regular Constitutional Convention was elected, and commenced its session on May 15, 1850. James H. Quinn was elected president of the convention. The convention sat for ten days and succeeded in formulating a Constitution which all concede to be an admirable instrument. It was dated May 25, and when printed was accompanied by an address, explanatory of some of its provisions as well as of the general advantages of Statehood, as excellent in its substance and tone as the Constitution itself.

The two features which naturally attract most attention are the clear declaration against slavery in the new State, and the appreciation shown of the value of public education. Besides the section of the Constitution forever prohibiting slavery in New Mexico, there was a strong paragraph on that subject in the accompanying address showing that slavery had always been the curse of the communities in which it existed.

It is an evidence of the courage and high principle of the convention which formulated the Constitution, that at that time, when the debate on slavery was raging in Congress, when they knew that the slave power was determined to have a new slave State to balance California, and that if they declared for slavery they would be admitted in a moment; they sacrificed their prospects of immediate admission to the higher duty of protecting their cherished land from the incubus and wrong of human bondage. It should never be forgotten that this first Constitutional Convention in New Mexico, in which native New Mexicans composed over ninety per cent. of the membership, took this high ground and maintained it courageously, although by so doing they were placing in jeopardy their own right to self government.

On May 28th, Col. Monroe, the Military Governor, issued his proclamation calling for an election on the adoption of the Constitution to be held on June 20th, and also a vote on a separate ballot "for governor, lieutenant governor, representative to Congress, and for senators and representatives to a State Legislature to convene at the capital on Monday the first day of July next. It being provided and understood that the election of all officers can only be valid by the adoption of a constitution by the people, and otherwise null and void; and that all action of the governor, lieutenant governor, and of the legislature shall remain inoperative until New Mexico be admitted as a State under said Constitution, except such acts as may be necessary for the primary steps of organization and the presentation of said Constitution properly before the Congress of the United States. The present government shall remain in full force until, by the action of Congress, another shall be substituted."

The proclamation was thus carefully worded in order to express the opinion of Gov. Monroe as to the effect of the election and the powers of the new State officials, an opinion to which he adhered without deviation to the end. In this the Military Governor of New Mexico differed widely from similar officials in California, where Gov. Riley in his proclamation of election clearly expressed his intention to surrender his authority to the new State Governor, if the Constitution should be adopted, and actually carried out that promise.

In New Mexico, there was no real contest over the Constitution, which seems to have been universally approved; the vote in favor of its adoption being 8,371 against 39 opposed. But for State and local officers there was the usual political contest. The candidates for governor and lieutenant or vice governor on one ticket were Henry Connelly, a well known merchant of the Santa Fe trail, and Manuel Alvarez, for many years U. S. Consul at Santa Fe; while opposed to them were Tomas Cabeza de Baca and Ceran St. Vrain. A few of the ballots used at this first State election are still in existence, in the collection of the New Mexico Historical Society, and are written on paper of uniform size. Those that are preserved were for Santa Fe County, and are "split" as to some of the candidates, being for Baca for Governor, and Alvarez for Vice-Governor, probably a popular combination in that locality. Connelly and Alvarez were elected by a considerable majority.

So strongly contested was this first State election that a contest was made before the Senate by Murray F. Tuley. Levi D. Keithley and Donaciano Vigil, claiming the seats for which Joseph Nangle, Domingo Baca and Jose F. Leiba received certificates from the district composed of Santa Fe, San Miguel and Santa Ana counties. This Murray F. Tuley was the same who afterwards achieved wide celebrity as a judge in Chicago, occupying the bench there for over a quarter of a century.

The legislature met on the 4th of July and continued in session over a week. It elected Francis A. Cunningham and Richard H. Weightman, United States Senators; made various appointments, ordered an election for local officials in August, organized the County of Socorro, and proceeded to enact general legislation. This was entirely contrary to the language of Gov. Monroe's proclamation, and assumed that the State was actually established, and its government fully organized, without any Congressional action.

A controversy immediately arose between Alvarez, acting as State Governor, while Connelly was absent in the east, and Col. Monroe, the Military and Civil Governor of the Territory. Both were able men and sustained their respective positions with vigor. On July 6th, Alvarez sent to Monroe a long defense of the course of the State government. He claimed that the people had a right to organize a civil government without consulting the military authorities; that any private citizen might have issued the proclamation; that in the absence of Congressional legislation, the people of New Mexico had as good a right to form or remodel their own system, or establish a new one, as the people of New York or Virginia; that Monroe's civil power could be no greater than that of the President, and that the President had never pretended to have the power to make a government for New Mexico or insist on the old one; that the President's instructions, and all others from Washington, simply advised temporary submission to the old government as existing by presumed consent of the people. That consent had been withdrawn and a new government organized, which must be recognized until Congress should refuse to sanction it."

On July 12th Col. Monroe answered, insisting on adherence to the terms of his original proclamation and on a continuance of the old regime pending Congressional action.

Gov. Alvarez immediately replied, deploring the controversy, but asserting that the people cannot surrender their dearest rights.

On the 15th, the Senate and House of the State Legislature passed resolutions endorsing the action of Gov. Alvarez, signed by W. Z. Angney, president of the Senate, and Joseph Nangle, speaker of the House.

On the 23rd, Col. Monroe, by Donaciano Vigil, Secretary of the Territory, sent a circular letter to the Prefects of all the counties, informing them that "the State government of New Mexico has no legal existence until New Mexico shall be admitted into the Union as a State by the Congress of the United States; and that, until otherwise deermined by competent authority, the present government continues and will be sustained."

As the time for the local elections under the State legislative Act approached, a compromise was effected in order to allay the popular excitement. The legislature adopted a joint resolution stating that "no officer, elective or appointive, under the State government, will attempt to exercise any jurisdicion until after November first or until duly commissioned to act as such"; and on August 9, Col. Monroe responded by another letter from Secretary Vigil to the Prefects, instructing them that no obstacle should be offered to, and no part taken in, the State election on the 12th, but that the officials elected were not to be recognized. Thus any real conflict was avoided, until the news arrived by the slow mails across the plains, that Congress had passed the so-called Compromise Measures of 1850, which settled the whole matter.

Under their provisions California was admitted as a free State; New Mexico and Utah, covering all the remaining area acquired from Mexico, were made into territories, with no mention of slavery; Texas abandoned her claim on New Mexico east of the Rio Grande, and received a large sum as compensation for that concession. These measures were signed by the President on September 9, 1850, and effectually ended the career of the new State of New Mexico and the work of the Convention in 1850. The two senators-elect had proceeded across the plains as far as Independence, Missouri, before they received the news which blighted their hopes of high official life.

William S. Meservey, who had been elected member of the House at the June election, continued his journey to Washington, and succeeded in being recognized and admitted as Delegate from the Territory instead of Representative of the State.

The President appointed James S. Calhoun first Governor of the New Territory under the Organic Act, and the entire territorial government was put into operation in March, 1851. The people settled down to a new order of things, and nothing was heard of Statehood for several years. Then came the great Rebellion, and the attention of the people was fully occupied in their defense against the invasion of the Texans and in the wars with the Indian tribes which practically encircled the Territory.

CHAPTER V.

LEGISLATIVE EFFORT AND CONSTITUTION OF 1872.

The next formal action looking towards Statehood was early in 1866, when the Legislature passed an act authorizing the Governor to call a Constitutional Convention, to be elected on the first Monday in March and to meet in the City of Santa Fe; the Constitution formulated to be submitted to a vote of the people on the fourth Monday in June. Apparently nothing of a practical nature was accomplished under this law.

On February 3, 1870, the Legislature passed an act providing for an election to be held on the first Monday in October of that year for the purpose of submitting a State constitution and electing the State officers and legislature provided for therein. The Governor was required to issue a proclamation for the election thirty days before its occurrence. The preamble to the Act reads as follows: "Whereas, We, the members of the Legislative Assembly of the Territory of New Mexico, as the representatives of the people, after due consideration of the best interests of New Mexico that the present circumstances and condition of the country will permit, have considered it best to submit for the consideration of the people, a constitution which appears to us proper and in which is embodied the fundamental principles of a free and sovereign State, etc." From this it appears that the Constitution had been already prepared when the Act was passed; but nothing seems to have resulted from this attempt to secure self-government.

To remedy this failure, the succeeding legislature took up the subject early in the session and passed a bill which was approved by the Governor on February 1, 1872, entitled "An Act providing for a General Election for the Purpose of Submitting to a Vote of the People a State Constitution and State Officers." After a Preamble which states, among other things that the Legislature is satisfied that a majority of the people desire a State Government, the law provided that a General Election should be held on the first Monday in June, 1872, "for the purpose of submitting to a vote of the people the State Constitution drafted at the present term of the Legislative Assembly."

Section five reads as follows: "If a majority of the votes cast be in favor of the Constitution and a State, the Governor is hereby required to issue his proclamation on the second Monday of July announcing the result of said election, and ordering another election, which shall be held on the first Monday in September, for the object of electing under said Constitution a Governor, Lieutenant Governor, Secretary of State, Auditor, Treasurer, Attorney General, Superintendent of Public Instruction, and also members of the Legislative Assembly and also a Representative to the Congress of the United States."

The Constitution that was thus submitted was printed in a pamphlet of forty-seven pages and was a comprehensive and well arranged document, creditable to those who prepared and adopted it.

For the purpose of showing the excellent character of this Constitution, fully abreast of the times and in every respect in advance of many of the Constitutions existing in 1872, the following sections are extracted:

CONSTITUTION OF 1872.
ART. IV.

Sec. 3. * * "No judge or clerk of any court, secretary of state, attorney general, state's attorney, recorder, sheriff or collector of public revenue, member of either house of congress, or person holding any lucrative office under the United States, this state, or any foreign government, shall have a seat in the General Assembly;"

PASSAGE OF BILLS.
ART. IV.

Sec. 6. * * "Every bill shall be read at large on three different days, in each house, and the bill, and all amendments thereto, shall be printed before the vote is taken on its final passage; and every bill having passed both houses shall be signed by the speakers thereof."

PRIVILEGES AND DISABILITIES.

"No person elected to the General Assembly shall receive any civil appointment within this state from the governor and senate, or from the General Assembly, during the term for which he shall have been elected, and all such appointments, and all votes given for any such members for any such office or appointment shall be void; nor shall any member of the General Assembly be interested, either directly or indirectly, in any contract with the state, or any county thereof, authorized by any law passed during the term for which he shall have been elected, or within one year after the expiration thereof."

PUBLIC MONEYS AND APPROPRIATIONS.

"No money shall be drawn from the treasury except in pursuance of an appropriation made by law, and on the presentation of an account issued by the auditor thereon; and no money shall be diverted from any appropriation made for any purpose, or taken from any fund whatever, either by joint or separate resolution."

"The General Assembly shall never grant or authorize extra compensation, fee or allowance to any public officer, agent, servant, or contractor, after service has been rendered, or a contract made; nor authorize the payment of any claim, or part thereof, hereafter created against the state under any agreement or contract made without express authority of law; and all such unauthorized agreements or contracts shall be null and void."

"The state shall never pay, assume or become responsible for the debts or liabilities of, or in any manner give, loan or extend its credit to or in aid of, any public or other corporation, association or individual."

SPECIAL LEGISLATION PROHIBITED.

"The General Assembly shall not pass local or special laws in any of the following enumerated cases, that is to say:

"For granting divorces; changing the names of persons or places; laying out, opening, altering and working roads or highways; vacating roads, town plots, streets and public grounds; locating or changing county seats; regulating county and township affairs; regulating the practice in courts of justice; regulating the jurisdiction and duties of justices of the peace, police magistrates and constables; providing for changes of venue in civil and criminal cases; incorporating cities, towns or villages, or changing or amending the charter of any city, town or village; summoning and empanneling grand or petit juries; providing for the management of common schools; regulating the interest on money; the opening or conducting of any election, or designating the place of voting; the sale or mortgage of real estate belonging to minors or others under disability; chartering or licensing ferries or toll bridges; remitting fines, penalties or forfeitures; creating, increasing or decreasing fees, percentage or allowance of public officers, during the term for which said officers are elected or appointed; changing the law of descent; granting to any corporation, association or individual any special or exclusive privilege, immunity or franchise whatever; granting to any corporation, association or individual the right to lay down railroad tracks, or amending existing charters for such purpose."

MISCELLANEOUS.

"The General Assembly shall have no power to authorize lotteries or gift enterprises for any purpose, and shall pass laws to prohibit the sale of lottery or gift-enterprise tickets in this state."

EDUCATION.

"Section 1. The General Assembly shall provide a thorough and efficient system of free schools whereby all the children of this state may receive a good common school education.

"Sec. 2. All lands, money or other property, donated, granted or received, for school, college, seminary or university purposes, and the proceeds thereof, shall be faithfully applied to the objects for which such gifts or grants were made.

Sec. 3. Neither the General Assembly, nor any county, city, town, township, school district or other public corporation shall ever make any appropriation, or pay from any public fund whatever, anything in aid of any church or sectarian purpose, or help, support or sustain any school, academy, seminary, college, university or other literary or scientific institution, controlled by any church or sectarian denomination whatever, nor shall any grant or donation of land, money or other personal property ever be made by the state or any such public corporation, to any church, or for any sectarian purpose.

"Sec. 4. No teacher, state, county, township, or district school officer, shall be interested in the sale, proceeds or profits of any book, apparatus or furniture, used or to be used in any school in this state with which such officer or teacher may be connected, under such penalties as may be provided by the General Assembly."

REVENUE.

"Sec. 12. No county, city, township, school district or other municipal corporation shall be allowed to become indebted in any manner, or for any purpose, to an amount, including existing indebtedness, in the aggregate exceeding five per centum on the value of the taxable property therein; to be ascertained by the last assessment for state and county taxes, previous to the incurring of such indebtedness."

COUNTY SEATS.

"No county seat shall be removed until the point to which it is proposed to be removed shall be fixed in pursuance of law, and a majority of the votes of the county to be ascertained in such manner as shall be provided by general law, shall have voted in favor of its removal to such point."

RAILROADS.

"Sec. 4. Railroads heretofore constructed or hereafter to be constructed in this state, are hereby declared public highways, and shall be free to all persons for the transportation of their persons and property thereon, under such regulations as may be prescribed by law. And the General Assembly shall pass such laws from time to time, establishing reasonable maximum rates of charges for the transporation of passengers and freight on the different railroads in this state.

"Sec. 5. No railroad corporation shall issue any stock or bonds except for money, labor or property actually received and applied to the purposes for which such corporation was created; and all stock dividends and other fictitious increase of the capital stock or indebtedness of any such corporation shall be void. The capital stock of no railroad corporation shall be increased for any purpose except upon giving sixty days public notice in such manner as may be provided by law.

"Sec. 6. The exercise of the power and right of eminent domain shall never be so construed or abridged as to prevent the taking by the General Assembly of the property and franchises of incorporated companies already organized, and subjecting them to the public necessity, the same as of individuals. The right of trial by jury shall be held inviolate in all trials of claims for compensation, when in the exercise of the said right of eminent domain any incorporated company shall be interested either for or against the exercise of said right.

"Sec. 7. The General Assembly shall pass laws to correct abuses and prevent unjust discriminations and extortion in the rates of freight and passenger tariffs on the different railroads in this state, and enforce such laws by adequate penalties, to the extent, if necessary for that purpose, of the forfeiture of their property and franchise."

JUDICIAL.

"Sec. 10. The justices of the supreme court and district judges, shall be ineligible to any office other than a judicial office, during the term for which they shall have been elected, and all elections or appointments of any such judges by the people, legislature, or otherwise, during such period, to any office other than judicial shall be void."

SCHEDULE.

"Sec. 10. For the first three years after the adoption of this constitution the legislature shall not levy a tax for state purposes exceeding one per cent per annum on the taxable property in the state."

In the large towns of the Territory much interest was taken in the Statehood election and the campaign which preceded it; but away from the centers of population the people were apathetic.

A large meeting of the citizens of central New Mexico was held at Albuquerque on May 12th, at which Col. J. Francisco Chaves presided and Candelario Garcia, Benjamin Stevens, Jose Armijo y Ortiz, Tranquilino Luna, etc., were conspicuous figures. Strong resolutions were passed favoring Statehood and the following resolution was included, protesting against the transfer of the strip of northern New Mexico to Colorado which afterwards took place.

"Resolved, That we will do all in our power, by all honorable means, to defeat the alarming scheme set on foot by citizens of Colorado, to annex six of our most populous counties to that Territory, so as to secure her admission as a State, on the plea that we are indifferent; that we are impelled to his course by our pride and our independence, and to prevent our people, our relations and our interests from becoming separated, divided and made tributary to a neighboring Territory; and we call on the people throughout the whole Territory, as they love their native soil, their homes, their wives and their children, as they esteem our interests, and to protect all they hold near and dear, to vote for our admission into the Union, and put the seal of condemnation and disapprobation on all such obnoxious plans and schemes."

(New Mexican, May 14th.)

In Santa Fe a similar meeting was held on May 26th, at which Antonio Ortiz y Salazar presided, and Major Jose D. Sena, Thomas F. Conway, Gaspar Ortiz, Jesus Maria Luna y Baca, Eben Everett, Dr. Andrews and others were conspicuous. Resolutions of the same character as those passed in Albuquerque were adopted, (New Mexican, May 28th).

The "New Mexican" of May 29th devoted a column and a half to a long article entitled "Reasons Why the People Should Adopt the State Constitution" which enumerated the following as among the objects to be attained by immediate Statehood:

"To avoid ruin, annexation to other territories, division of our people, our interests, and separation of our relatives; to sustain our pride, our independence, and our history, the oldest in the United States; to protect our interests, induce prosperity and transmit blessings we have not enjoyed to our children; to secure a proper State organization and insure good and wholesome legislation adapted to our wants; to have the privilege of abrogating, changing or amending existing laws, that are unjust, odious and oppressive, and correcting existing evils; to manage our own affairs and select our own officers, in fine, to make us a happy, intelligent, enterprising and prosperous people; vote for the Constitution and the State."

Notwithstanding the meetings and activities of committees, the actual vote on election day was so small as to disappoint those interested. There was really nothing strange in this. Not specially in New Mexico, but everywhere when an abstract question is to be voted upon or the personal element does not enter into the campaign, the ordinary vote is cut down to a comparatively small fraction of the ordinary normal vote.

On the day after the election the Daily New Mexican said "the election yesterday passed off very quietly, only about half of the vote being polled." It was not till June 10th that the vote of Santa Fe County was finally announced, being 554 in favor of the Constitution and 346 against; giving a majority of 208. In the city of Santa Fe the vote was 424 in favor and 77 against.

The next day there appeared in the New Mexican an editorial article, evidently inspired by Gov. Giddings, which gave a reason or rather an excuse for letting the whole subject drop. As the law was mandatory and absolutely required the Governor to issue the proclamation for a State election on the second Monday in July, if the June vote was in favor of Statehood, this affords another example of the evil results of the system under which officials are not responsible to the people and are too often regardless of law.

The article is as follows:

"We understand that the election to vote on the Constitution has gone substantially by default. By an error in fixing the time too short in which to make returns, many of the counties have made none. One county, in which there is a very large population, with sixteen or seventeen precincts, returned votes only for one precinct, giving all for the State and not a single one against it. In a large number of precincts no election was held at all, and it is said this was in consequence of the general belief that Congress would not admit us as a State, and therefore there was no propriety in going through the farce of an election for State officers, at a great expense, unless Congress should first authorize it and show its willingness to admit us. This feeling was intensified by the fact that only a few days since one branch of Congress laid on the table the bill heretofore introduced for the same purpose. All these things combined to prevent any fair expression of the sentiment of the people. And while the probability now is that the votes which have been cast will show a fair majority in favor of the Constitution and State, yet we understand that the Governor, upon looking at the whole vote cast, which will not probably exceed one-third of the real vote of the Territory, does not feel authorized to call an election and make the Territory a great bill of expense. If a majority of the voters in the Territory had voted on the question, we think the ruling would have been different; but if the fact turns out to be that only one-third of the voters turned out, then we question, much as we favor a state organization, the propriety of calling an election for State officers, even though a majority of the votes cast are in favor of the Constitution." (New Mexican, June 11th, 1872).

So this attempt at Statehood, which occupied the attention of two legislatures, caused a Constitution to be prepared, printed, approved by the legislature, and submitted to the people at a special election held solely for that purpose, died, without any good cause.

And another of the unfortunate accidents which have retarded the progress of New Mexico was added to the list.

The succeeding legislature, which met in December, 1873, gave official voice to the public desire by passing a Memorial to the U. S. Senate and House of Representatives strongly urging Congressional action "for the immediate admission of this Territory as a State"; that being the most proper and effective method of procedure, as a Statehood bill was then under consideration in the national legislature at Washington.

CHAPTER VI.

CONGRESSIONAL ACTION TO 1876.

While these proceedings had been taken in New Mexico, on almost every available occasion, Congress had been no less active in considering the subject.

At almost every session a bill for the admission of New Mexico was introduced, generally reported favorably in the House, and more or less considered, but without any definite result.

In 1869 an attempt was made, though not by New Mexicans, to transform the Territory into a State called Lincoln; but this project was ultimately defeated in the Senate.

In the 40th Congress, Delegate J. Francisco Chaves made a vigorous and eloquent speech in favor of Statehood and in defense of the people against unjust criticism,

In the 43rd Congress (1873-5) the Enabling Act was introduced by Hon. Stephen B. Elkins, then Delegate from New Mexico, and now Senator from West Virginia, and on the 21st of May, 1874, he delivered a carefully prepared speech on the bill, which contained the best collection of facts and arguments on the subject that had ever been presented to Congress. He claimed 130,000 inhabitants for the Territory, exclusive of Pueblo Indians, showed that at least fifteen States had been admitted to the Union with a smaller population, laid stress on the smallness of the public debt and presented a vivid picture of her great natural resources. He then took up the question of the obligation on the part of the government to grant Statehood to New Mexico arising from General Kearny's pledges and the Treaty of Guadalupe Hidalgo, and closed with a well-deserved tribute to the patriotism, loyalty and law-abiding character of the people.

The bill passed the House by the remarkable vote of 160 to 54 and was sent to the Senate for concurrence. In that body it was carefully considered in committee and open session, and finally passed on February 24, 1875, by the decisive majority of 32 to 11, with a slight amendment. Running parallel with it in both Houses was the bill to admit Colorado, almost identical in language, introduced and championed by Hon. Thomas M. Patterson, then Delegate from that Territory and since Senator. While the vote was nearly the same for the two bills, the one for New Mexico had a slight advantage in majority down to the time when both passed the Senate with identical amendments. It was then that the series of misadventures which had accompanied all the attempts to secure New Mexican Statehood from the beginning, culminated in the incident which has become historic as the "Elkins handshake," and again dashed the cup of success from the very lips of the people of the Territory.

THE ELKINS' HANDSHAKE.

This incident has been narrated scores of times in slightly varying form, not only as an interesting item of current history but a remarkable illustration of the way in which insignificant and unintentional acts, sometimes change the course of very important events. The story may be briefly told as follows: Mr. Elkins was possessed of a most cordial manner, an ever-present expansive smile, and a warmth of greeting, which were among the causes of his personal popularity, and which advancing age and senatorial dignity have not yet obliterated. This charm of manner had made many friends even among political opponents, and among those whose support for the New Mexico Statehood Bill he had thus secured on its passage by the House, were a considerable number of Representatives from Georgia and Alabama. When the bill was returned to the House, after passing the Senate with amendments on February 24th, but ten days of the session remained, and the difficulty was not to secure concurrence in the Senate amendments, which were unobjectionable, but to get the bill before the House for action within this brief and busy time. To suspend the rules required a two-thirds vote, and this was necessary if the bill was to be considered at all.

Just at this time, Hon. Julius C. Burroughs, of Michigan, made a powerful speech on political subjects, in which he characterized the Rebellion and those engaged in it in plain terms,—what at that period, on account of its allusions to the War, was called a "bloody shirt" speech. Mr. Elkins, who had been conversing with friends in the lobby, had not heard a word of the speech, but happened to re-enter the Chamber just as Mr. Burroughs had concluded and was receiving the congratulations of a crowd of members about him. Filled with his spirit of cordiality, Mr Elkins joined the group and shook hands with the speaker with characteristic vigor. This was observed by a number of southern members, whose feelings had been much excited by the speech, and they instantly concluded that they would lend no aid to the passage of the New Mexico bill which it was understood would bring Mr. Elkins speedily to the Senate. The Delegate himself was entirely ignorant of any change in their views or of having done anything to arouse their opposition, until George Q. Cannon, Delegate from Utah, learned the facts and informed him. He did what he could in the brief interval to repair the damage, but a sufficient number of former supporters, from Georgia and Alabama, refused to be placated, to make it impossible to obtain the two-thirds vote necessary; and so the Enabling Act was lost for lack of opportunity to obtain concurrence by the House in the Senate amendments. More than thirty-five years have passed since that day and New Mexico still remains a Territory on account of that impulsive and unconsidered handshake.

CHAPTER VII.

CONGRESSIONAL ACTION 1876 TO 1895.

In the succeeding Congress (the 44th) Mr. Elkins again secured the introduction of the Enabling Act for New Mexico, and it passed the Senate, during its first session, on March 10th, 1876, by the strong vote of 35 to 15. In the House of Representatives, it was reported favorably by the Committee on Territories, and was on the calendar, awaiting action at the time of the final adjournment.

After these virtual defeats,—although in no case was there an actual vote adverse to New Mexico, and the retirement of Mr. Elkins as Delegate, no active efforts looking to Statehood were made for several years. The approach of the railroad, and its actual arrival in 1879; followed by the influx of a new population, the establishment of new towns, and the general mining excitement which extended over the entire Territory in the early '80s, seem to have occupied the thought and attention of the people; and during the Congressional terms of Trinidad Romero, Mariano S. Otero, Tranquilino Luna and F. A. Manzanares, and the earlier years of Antonio Joseph, no effective efforts were made in Washington looking to the admission of New Mexico to the Union. During most of this period, Dakota, with its rapidly increasing population, was vainly endeavoring to secure Statehood, and being most unjustly excluded for political reasons; and it was obviously impossible for any less populous Territory to be admitted until her urgent application was heeded.

Early in the first session of the 50th Congress, which met in December, 1887, a bill was introduced "To provide for the formation and admission into the Union of the States of Washington, Dakota, Montana and New Mexico", designated as H. R. 4431.

Previous to this, separate bills had been introduced for the admission of Dakota and (H. R. 1276), Montana (H. R. 1955), and Washington, (H. R. 4430). The committee on territories, to which they were all referred, reported on March 13, 1888, House Bill No. 8466, a substitute for the entire four bills, entitled "A Bill to Enable the People of Dakota, Montana, Washington and New Mexico to Form Constitutions and State Governments and to be Admitted into the Union on an Equal Footing with the Original States."

With regard to New Mexico it contained one peculiar section which reads as follows:

Sec. 20. That the constitutional convention to assemble in the Territory of New Mexico, as hereinbefore provided, shall submit to the people as a separate proposition to be voted upon at the same time that the vote upon the constitution is taken, the question of changing the name of the State from that of the State of New Mexico to that of the State of Montezuma, and if a majority of voters shall be in the affirmative, the name of the State shall, upon its admission, be Montezuma; and all the powers, rights, privileges, grants, and obligations pertaining under this act to the State of New Mexico shall attach to, be vested in, and imposed upon the State of Montezuma."

The entire elimination of New Mexico from the bill before its final passage, of course deprived this section of any practical importance, but it is interesting as a matter of history.

Accompanying this bill was a very voluminous report, or series of reports, covering 145 pages and containing much information and many contradictory opinions regarding the four territories affected by it. This is known as Report No. 1025, 50th Congress, 1st Session. The majority report was made by Mr. Springer, chairman of the committee, and considers the case of each of the territories in turn, the principal portion being devoted to Dakota and an argument in favor of its admission as one State instead of two. It excuses the outrageous conduct of Congress in not admitting Dakota. with its great populaion, years before, by laying the blame on the people of that Territory, who were insisting that the interests of the two sections of Dakota were so diverse, that it should be divided into two States, by a line running east and west through its center, much as was ultimately done by the creation of North and South Dakota.

The report estimates the population of the four territories as follows:

Dakota 568,000
Montana 175,000
Washington 160,000
New Mexico 150,000

The portion of the report devoted to New Mexico gives a brief history of its previous attempts to be admitted to the Union; refers to its great resources and the marked progress in its actual industries; quotes the memorial of the Legislature asking for Statehood; and in proof of the present desire of the people, cites the recent expressions of opinion published in the "New Mexican." That newspaper shortly before, in order to ascertain public opinion on the subject, had addressed circular letters to a large number of leading citizens asking for their views as to Statehood. Replies were received from 122 persons, who represented every county in the Territory. Of these 91 were in favor of, and 31 against, immediate admission. Of the 91 in favor, 41 were republicans, 33 democrats and 17 of unknown politics. Of the 31 opposed, 11 were democrats, 10 republicans, 6 of no particular politics, and 4 who called themselves independent. So that the division was not at all along party lines. A classification by kinds of business also failed to develop unanimous approval or opposition in any particular avocation, although the lawyers consulted were nearly all in favor of Statehood. It is to be remembered that no bill relating to New Mexico had been referred to the committee, and the inclusion of that Territory in the bill was an act of justice and grace on the part of the committee, largely attributed to Mr. Springer, who was well acquained with the country and its people.

The minority report, presented by Mr. Struble of Iowa, attracted much attention, and aroused great indignation in New Mexico, on account of its violent opposition to our admission to Statehood, and the bitter attack on the Territory and its people. It insisted that Dakota should be divided into two States and adduced excellent reasons therefor; agreed with the majority in recommending Montana and Washington; and reserved all of its criticism for New Mexico. It calls the action of the committee in recommending Statehood, a "surprising and unjustifiable attempt," especially as "neither the Delegate, nor Governor Ross, who was in Washington during most of the session, has urged any action by Congress."

It then quotes from a number of supposed "authorities", the quotations always being of an unfavorable nature. Thus it makes this extraordinary historical discovery from Gaskell's Atlas, relating to Santa Fe, "The Spaniards found this a populous town in 1542. Its history is one long continued strife between the cruel and hated Spaniards and the native Pueblos." Considering that no Spaniard was there in 1542, nor for 60 years afterwards, and that there has been no Pueblo trouble for over 200 years, the value of that extract is easily estimated.

Then it quotes from one McCabe, who said of the same city: "It is wretchedly built. The houses are constructed of adobe and are one story in height. The inhabitants, with the exception of a few Americans residing in the place, are ignorant and degraded. The place bears an evil reputation as one of the most reckless and miserable towns on the globe."

Then follows a long extract from "El Gringo," which was written more than thirty years before, under entirely different conditions; and a quotation from Prof. Bliss, principally concerning the Penitentes.

These are followed by an unfavorable view of education in the Territory, and extracts from the reports of Governors Wallace and Sheldon reflecting on the primitive style of agriculture employed and from the last report of Gov. Ross severely criticising the methods of legislation and denouncing the "viciousness of the schemes of personal hatred and of plunder that characterized nearly every one of the sixty days of the life of the last session." The whole is supplemented by the question "'is it not apparent that the people of New Mexico are not yet prepared for intelligent, honest and capable management of State government?"

The subject was discussed at length, both in and out of Congress, and the result was the elimination of New Mexico and the admission of the two Dakotas as separate States, of Washington and Montana.

As New Mexico was dropped from the Omnibus Bill in which it had originally been included, a separate Act became necessary, and, on Feb. 15, 1889, near the end of the 50th Congress, Hon. Antonio Joseph, Delegate from New Mexico, introduced House Bill No. 12,592, an Enabling Act for the Territory of New Mexico alone, entitled: "A bill to enable the people of New Mexico to form a constitution and State government and to be admitted into the Union on an equal footing with the original States," which was referred to the Committee on Territories of the House and the next day reported and committed to the Committee of the Whole House on the State of the Union, and ordered printed. Of course it was then too late in the session for any hope of successful action; but it kept the subject officially before Congress, and showed the continued desire of the Territory for admission.

This bill contained the following peculiar provision, which was probably an attempt to introduce the name of "Montezuma" by indirection, so that it would not meet with opposition in Congress, but could be arranged by argument and influence in the convention. Whoever was behind the movement entirely misunderstood the prevailing sentiment in New Mexico, or underrated its strength, as is more fully shown elsewhere.

"Sec. 21. That the constitutional convention to assemble in the Territory of New Mexico, as hereinbefore provided, shall submit to the people, as a separate proposition, to be voted upon at the same time that the vote upon the Constitution is taken, the question of changing the name of the State from that of the State of New Mexico to that name for the proposed State which said convention may select and indicate, and if a majority of voters shall be in the affirmative the name of the State shall, upon its admission, be changed accordingly; and all the powers, rights, privileges, grants, and obligations pertaining under this Act to the State of New Mexico shall attach to, be vested in, and imposed upon the State by the name thus selected and adopted."

The report on this bill made by Mr. Springer on behalf of the committee, on Feb. 16th, 1889, (Report No. 4090, 50th Congress, 2nd Session), contains the same argument in favor of the admission of New Mexico that was in the majority report on the Omnibus Bill previously referred to; and in addition a large amount of matter showing the recent educational progress of New Mexico, and an interesting statement by Maj. Powell as to the enormous area of land which can be added to the agricultural area of the territory by storage reservoirs and irrigation.

At the beginning of the next session of Congress, in the succeeding December, 1889, this being the first session of the 51st Congress, of which Hon. Antonio Joseph was again a member from New Mexico, enjoying his third term of service,—Mr. Joseph, on December 18, 1889, introduced House Bill No. 968 which was practically the same as his bill of Feb. 15, 1889, but omitted section 21 of the latter which had directed the constitutional convention to submit to the people, as a separate proposition, a new name for the proposed State, to be selected by the convention.

In order to take advantage of any opportunity that might be presented for the passage of this bill in the Senate, if that should be possible before action in the House, Senator Wolcott of Colorado, introduced in the Senate, on Feb. 4, 1890, the same bill, which was designated "S. 2446," and referred to the Committee on Territories.

In the meantime on the 6th day of January, 1890, Mr. Springer, of Illinois, introduced a bill (H. R. 3830) "To enable the people of Arizona, Idaho, New Mexico and Wyoming, to form constitutions and State governments and to be admitte into the Union," etc. This embodied the usual provisions, together with an original one, which has subsequently found a place in succeeding bills and forms part of the Act of 1910; being the section which authorizes the re-convening of the Constitutional Convention and the forming and submission of a second Constitution, in case the first one framed shall be rejected by the people.

In this case, again, the Southwest was neglected and the Northwest was favored; for before the passage of the bill, Arizona and New Mexico, though by far the oldest of the four territories named, and New Mexico being also the most populous, were eliminated from it. They were thus left in the territorial condition, while Idaho and Wyoming, with a combined population less than that of New Mexico alone, were admitted.

On April 3rd, 1890, Mr. Joseph took advantage of the consideration of the bill for the admission of Idaho, to make a speech relative to Statehood for New Mexico. He drew attention to the fact that the House had just passed the bill for the admission of Wyoming and was about to do the same for Idaho, and he proceeded to demonstrate that New Mexico had far better claims to Statehood than either of those territories. He urged the passage of the Enabling Act introduced by him early in the Session, but he opposed admission under the Constitution framed by the Constitutional Convention of 1889, on account of the partisan character of the convention. This evidence of a divided sentiment among the people, and that details and incidental matters were by some considered more important than the attainment of self-government itself, naturally weakened the cause of Statehood in the House rather than gave it strength.

In the 52nd Congress (1891-3), Mr. Joseph again introduced an Enabling Act, known as House Bill 7136. He succeeded in securing a favorable report from the Committee on Territories, and by courtesy was appointed to make the report himself, which he did on March 16, 1892. It contained 45 pages, closely printed, and appeared as Report No. 736, 52nd Cong., 1st Sess. The bill provided for an election, on the usual election day in November, 1892, of 75 delegates to form a Constitutional Convention;

and that the convention should assemble on the first Monday in December. It contained liberal donations of land for various purposes.

The report, besides the usual statements of area, population, etc., drew attention to the large expenditures already made by the Territory for public buildings, amounting to $600,000, and to the passage on March 3rd, 1891, of the Act to Establish a Court of Private Land Claims, which was expected to clear up all the unsettled titles of land grants in the Territory. It embodied the whole of the pamphlet issued by the Bureau of Immigration called "New Mexico the Coming Country," which contained a very full description of the resources and progress of New Mexico; and also the entire report of the hearing by the House Committee on Territories, on April 30, 1890, of the Committee of Fifty headed by Gov. Prince, elsewhere referred to; as well as the latest report of the Territorial Superintendent of Public Instruction. These constituted a very full and important document, which bore witness in all its parts to the worthiness of the Territory and people to be accorded the right of self government. But like all the preceding attempts, nothing practical resulted in that Congress, although considerable progress was made.

The bill passed the House on June 6th and reached the Senate June 8th, 1892, and there Senator Carey of Wyoming, who had had a long experience in a Territory, before Statehood brought to him the Senatorial toga, took charge of it. It was somewhat amended in the Senate Committee on Territories, the material alterations being a change in the dates of the election, convention, etc., making them dependent on the time of the passage of the bill; apportioning the delegates directly to the respective counties; somewhat reducing the land appropriations; and changing the provision with regard to the language of the public schools, from "in all of which schools the English language shall be taught" to "the said schools shall always be conducted in English." It was then reported to the Senate, favorably, on July 21, 1892 (Report No. 1023).

At the second Session of the 52nd Congress, Senator

Carey introduced in the committee on Jan. 28, 1893, two proposed amendments to this bill, intended to meet the cases of the other territories that were anxious for Statehood, and apparently arranged so as to attract the largest possible vote to the original measure, and to bring about the admission of as many territories as Congress should be willing to favor at that time.

Amendment No. 1 provided for the formation of four new States, New Mexico, Utah, Arizona and Oklahoma; the latter to include the Indian Territory.

Amendment No. 2 provided for the formation of three new States, New Mexico, Utah, and Oklahoma; being similar to No. 1, except the omission of Arizona.

That was within three weeks of the end of the Congress, and as might have been expected, no definite action was taken on these amendments, although Senator Carey made a very strong effort to have the bill amended about the middle of February, but was unable to obtain the two-third vote necessary; and thus nothing tangible was accomplished for the cause of Statehood in New Mexico.

In the 53rd Congress, Hon. Antonio Joseph was again a delegate from New Mexico, and introduced a Statehood bill at the earliest possible opportunity of the first session. It was known as House Bill No. 353, "An Act to Enable the People of New Mexico to Form a Constitution and State Government," etc. The title by this time had become almost stereotyped. It was very similar in its provisions to the previous bill, providing for a convention of 75 delegates, who were apportioned among the counties in the bill; the election to be in November, 1894, and the convention to commence in December. One special feature was an appropriation of 500,000 acres of land for the establishment of permanent water reservoirs for irrigation purposes.

This bill passed the House on the 28th of June, 1894, and was received in the Senate June 29th and referred to the Committee on Territories.

On August 3, 1894, Senator Blackburn, of Kentucky, reported the bill favorably, with a few amendments. These changed the dates, as the original ones had proved to be too early, but did not alter the general tenor of the bill. As usual, the second session proved too short for action on the bill, and so it suffered the fate of its predecessors.

A little incident of hitherto unwritten history may be narrated here, because it presents another illustration of the chapter of accidents which have accompanied the "Struggle for Statehood" from the beginning and unexpectedly brought disappointment and failure on so many occasions.

On the very first day when bills could be introduced, the Enabling Acts for New Mexico and Utah were presented, the former by Mr. Joseph and the latter by the delegate from the Mormon Territory. Both were repetitions of old measures and were almost immediately reported from the committee; the New Mexico bill being just in advance of the one relating to Utah. Each delegate was anxiously awaiting the time when the bills should be reached on the Calendar and taken up for action, as they were determined to have them passed and sent to the Senate as early as possible. It was not supposed that they could be reached for action before the usual holiday recess. Just at this time, about the middle of December, Mr. Joseph suffered from a malarial attack, and believed that a few days at his home would dispel the trouble and bring him to good fighting condition for the expected contest. He consulted several leading members of the House, and they all concurred in the belief that there was no chance of reaching the bills before the recess, and consequently no danger incurred by absence at that time. So Mr. Joseph started for the salubrious climate of New Mexico in order to recuperate in the interval.

But it happened that Congress just then had one of its periodical fits of special industry. A serious attempt was made to omit the recess altogether and that was only defeated by postponing the recess until the day before Christmas and agreeing to work assiduously in the meantime. Thus the business was expedited far beyond all calculations, and just before the holidays the two Statehood bills were unexpectedly reached. The New Mexico one was first called, but as the delegate was not present to ask for its consideration, it lost its opportunity. The Utah bill was announced, and its sponsor succeeded in having it passed by the House then and there; and when Congress re-convened after the holidays it was in the Senate ready for reference. Sometime after, the New Mexico bill was again reached in the House and was passed with little difficulty. In fact, it had always been sure of more votes than the one for the admission of Utah, against which there was considerable prejudice and opposition on account of Mormonism. But the delay in time caused the difference in their fate.

The Utah bill was passed and became a law, under which a Constitutional Convention was held and the State admitted.

The New Mexico bill, though strongly advocated, never reached the point of being voted upon in the Senate.

No fault is attributed to Mr. Joseph, who was an earnest advocate of the bill and anxious for its success, and who had every reason to believe that his short absence would be harmless; but this adds another to the series of mishaps which have become proverbial.

CHAPTER VIII.

CONSTITUTION OF 1890.

While Congress was discussing in the Committee on Territories of the House the Enabling Act (House Bill 12,-592), introduced by Mr. Joseph, and just before Hon. W. R. Springer, of Illinois, the chairman of the committee, made his favorable report thereon, the people of New Mexico determined to take the matter into their own hands and initiate the necessary proceedings for admission to the Union.

In February, 1889, Hon. George W. Prichard of San Miguel County, introduced in the Council "An Act to Provide for a Constitutional Convention and the Formation of a State Constitution."

After various recitals by way of preamble, among which was the following emphatic one,

"Whereas, a territorial system of government is the most unsatisfactory that can be devised, being a government without stability, is temporary and uncertain in its character, possesses no sovereign powers, and fails to meet the requirements of the people," the bill provided for a delegate convention to be held in September, 1889, for the purpose of framing a Constitution. The convention was to be composed of 73 delegates, who were apportioned by the bill among the various counties, and were to be chosen at an election on the first Tuesday in August. It was to frame a constitution and provide for a special election at which such constitution should be submitted to the people for ratification. This bill was passed by both Houses, but the Governor failed to approve it, as he considered the apportionment objectionable; but he did not veto it, and it became a law by limitation, Feb. 28, 1889.

From the beginning, the Democratic leaders expressed dissatisfaction with the apportionment, which they asserted gave too much representation to republican counties; and perhaps there was some merit in their objection. They claimed to be favorable to Statehood and simply opposed to an unfair inequality. There was much talk of making some equitable arrangement whereby the parties' strength would be more equally balanced in the convention, and this resulted in calling the two party territorial committees to meet on the same day at Santa Fe. The most earnest Statehood men on both sides were anxious for some arrangement which would ensure the support of both parties for the Constitution.

The two committees met on June 12th, 1889, the attendance on both sides being good and composed of leading citizens. The republican committee took the lead by passing the following resolution:

"Whereas, the important question now before the people is the attainment of Statehood, and the result of the present efforts depends largely on the character of the convention and Constitution, and also on the united action of all good citizens without regard to party or other differences, therefore,

"Resolved, That the Republican Territorial Committee appoint a conference committee of three members to request the appointment by the Democratic Territorial Committee of a similar commitee, to confer as to the best method of electing the most eminent and best qualified citizens as members of the Constitutional Convention and interesting all men of patriotism and progress in the effort for Statehood;" and appointed as its committee Hon. L. B. Prince, Hon. M. S. Otero and Col. G. W. Prichard.

The Democratic committee accepted the invitation, and appointed Hon. F. A. Manzanares, C. H. Gildersleeve and W. B. Childers as their representatives. It was conceded without question that the Republican majority under the apportionment would be about 27, and that thta was more than it should equitably be. At the conference, after a friendly discussion, the Republicans consented to accept a majority of seven. The Democrats offered to concede three. The Republicans objected that three was too small a margin, as sickness or absence might destroy the majority. Apparently a compromise, giving five majority, was on the point of being arranged, when one of the Democratic conferees suddenly destroyed all hope of agreement by exclaiming excitedly "Our friends in Congress will never be satisfied unless we have half the convention." He seemed suddenly possessed by this idea; and so the conference failed. These particulars are narrated in order to show what a small matter again intervened to cause long delay in the struggle for statehood. But for the sudden, impetuosity of one man, followed by the persistent opposition of one other, the constitution of 1890 would surely have been adopted, and New Mexico admitted to the Union twenty years ago.

The plan for co-operation having failed, but one course remained open and the Republicans called county conventions to nominate candidates. At the same time the Territorial Committee expressed its regret at the failure, and as late as June 24th, Mr. W. W. Griffin, chairman of the committee, made a new effort for an arrangement, while the "New Mexican" vigorously advocated any fair adjustment of the differences.

The Democrats, as a rule, under peremptory orders from Mr. Childers, chairman of their committee, refused to nominate candidates or participate in the election. A very few men of sufficient influence or independence to disregard the commands of the party leaders, united with the Republicans in the campaign; Hon. L. S. Trimble, long a member of Congress from Kentucky, being the most conspicuous example. He was among the delegates subsequently elected from Bernalillo county.

On June 24th the Governor issued the usual proclamation of election, the time for holding which was Tuesday, Aug. 6th; but the Democratic Board of County Commissioners of Lincoln County endeavored to nullify the law by inaction, so far as their county was concerned, and nearly succeeded in doing so. Legal proceedings having failed, finally, on August 3rd, the Governor issued the following proclamation addressed to the voters of Lincoln County, which recited the facts and called on the people to exercise their rights.

"To the Legal Voters of Lincoln County:

The legislature of New Mexico, by Chap. 99, of the Laws of 1899, provided that an election should be held on Tuesday, August 6th, 1899, for the choice of delegates to a Constitutional Convention to be held in September of this year. By said Act the County Commissioners of the several counties are required to issue notices of election and do all other things necessary in the premises.

The County Commissioners of Lincoln County neglected and refused to perform their duties under said Act and thereupon the Court issued a peremptory writ of mandamus commanding said commissioners to meet and perform the duties required of them by law.

Information has been received that two of said commissioners absented themselves from said county and so escaped service of said writ, and still neglect and refuse to perform their duties, and that, therefore, no judges of election have yet been appointed for the several precincts of Lincoln County.

Now, therefore, I, L. Bradford Prince, Governor of New Mexico, do proclaim and make known:

1. That the right of the qualified citizens of New Mexico to vote at a territorial election cannot be destroyed by any illegal action or neglect of an officer in regard to such election.

2. That in accordance with law, an election will be held in the several precincts of Lincoln County on Tuesday, the sixth day of August, 1889.

3. That in pursuance of Sec. 1136 of the Compiled Laws of 1884, a majority of the qualified voters in each precinct have power to appoint judges who shall conduct said election in the same manner and to the same effect as if they had been appointed by the County Commissioners as provided by law.

I therefore recommend that the legal voters in each precinct assemble at the usual place of voting therein, at nine o'clock, on the morning of August 6th, or as soon thereafter as practicable, and that those so assembled then and there appoint judges as aforesaid.

And I advise the people of the respective precincts, if there shall be time for such action, to apply to the Probate Clerk for poll books and ballot boxes; and in cases in which they cannot be procured to provide suitable books and boxes, and in all things to conduct said election as nearly as practicable in conformity with the forms of law.

And as a matter of precaution I recommend that duplicate records of said election be sent direct to the Secretary of the Territory at Santa Fe.

Dated August 3, 1889.

       L. BRADFORD PRINCE,
         Governor of New Mexico.

By the Governor: B. M. Thomas,
    Secretary of the Territory."

Under this proclamation three of the most efficient delegates to the convention, Messrs. Terrell, Eddy and Heman, were elected.

The names of the members of the convention were as follows:—Bernalillo County: E. S. Stover, Alejandro Sandoval, R. Haberland, W. C. Hazledine, L. S. Trimble, Marcos C. de Baca, Bernard S. Rodey, Mariano S. Otero, Pedro Perea, Perfecto Armijo.

Colfax: A. C. Voorhees, Nestor Martinez, Cristobal Sanchez, E. W. Fox.

Dona Ana: A. J. Fountain, W. L. Rynerson, Martin Lohman.

Grant: John D. Bail, Warren Bristol, R. P. Hart.

Lincoln: S. S. Terrell, C. B. Eddy, T. W. Heman.

Mora: Severino Trujillo, C. W. Wildenstein, Mateo Lujan, Trinidad Romero.

Rio Arriba: J. M. C. Chavez, Jose Y. Esquibel, W. F. Burns, E. K. Caldwell, Pedro Y. Jaramillo, W. D. Lee.

Santa Fe: Nicolas Pino, P. L. VanderVeer, Aniceto Abeytia, J. D. Sena, T. B. Catron, F. W. Clancy.

Sierra: R. M. White, Nicholas Galles.

San Miguel: Pascual Baca, E. C. Winters, Manuel C. de Baca, E. F. Hobart, John G. Clancy, Jefferson Reynolds, Edward Henry, Leandro Sanchez, Romulo Ulibarri, G. W. Prichard, W. H. Shupp, Frank Springer.

San Juan: L. R. S. Paulin, David E. Lobato.

Socorro: Jacinto Sanchez, J. A. Whitmore, William E. Kelley, Jose Baca y Sedillo, Demetrio Perez, W. G. Ritch.

Taos: Antonio Martinez, Juan Martin, Antonio Roibal, Juan Trujillo, Francisco Duran, Manuel Chacon.

Valencia: Desiderio Sandoval, E. A. Dow, Patrocinio Luna, Juan Jose Benavides, Silvestrè Mirabal.

It met on September 3rd, 1889, elected J. Francisco Chaves as president and Ira M. Bond as secretary, and continued in session till September 21. The constitution was then printed in both English and Spanish and circulated widely throughout the Territory.

After an adjournment of nearly an entire year the convention re-assembled on August 18, 1890, and continued in session on that and the succeeding day, making a few amendments which had been suggested during the year, and providing for the submission of the Constitution to a vote of the people on October 7, 1890. It then adjourned sine die.

Under the direction of the officers of the convention a new edition of the proposed Constitution, as amended, was published in both of the languages current in the Territory, accompanied by a manifesto to the people setting forth the reasons for its adoption.

Between the adjournment of the convention and the time of the election a vigorous campaign was conducted all over the Territory. A Democratic convention, held at Silver City, declared against the Constitution and advised its adherents to oppose it, principally on four grounds:

1. That the appellate judges are to be appointed.
2. That the Governor is suspended during impeachment.
3. That the State tax is limited to one per cent.
4. That the apportionment is unjust.

This was followed up by a circular on the same general subjects signed by W. B. Childers, chairman, and Felix Martinez, secretary of the Democratic Territorial Committee.

The Republican Territorial Committee promptly responded with a circular answering the objections and ending with this exhortation: "In conclusion we beg of you, people of New Mexico, to give no heed to the lying misrepresentations of the enemies of progress. Read the Constitution for yourselves and consider whether any constitution ever framed could escape with less of criticism if it were subjected for more than a year to the careful examination of enemies. For the fact is not to be lost sight of, that the men who are active in their opposition are the same who were unfriendly before the convention met; who refused to participate in the election of delegates; who predicted that a quorum of the convention would never assemble; who attempted to cast ridicule on the proceedings of the convention while its sessions continued; who, in short, pre-judged everything, and in advance pledged themselves to fight against whatever might be the result of the labors of the convention." This was signed by S. B. Axtell, chairman, and L. A. Hughes, secretary of the committee.

Meetings were held in all parts of the Territory, Gov. Axtell, Col. J. F. Chaves, Gov. Stover, Judge Trimble, Maj. Sena, Hon. T. B. Catron, Hon. A. L. Morrison, Col. H. L. Pickett, Col. Rynerson, Hon. M. S. Otero, R. E. Twitchell, E A. Fiske, J. H. Knaebel and others speaking in favor of the Constitution, and, W. B. Childers, H. B. Fergusson, Felix Martinez, N. B. Field, C. H. Gildersleeve, J. H. Crist, N. B. Laughlin, Gov. Ross, etc., opposing its adoption. The campaign was opened by a great procession and meeting in the Plaza at Santa Fe, called by the Press at the time "the largest and most brilliant public demonstration ever held in New Mexico," at which Judge Axtell presided and Gov. Prince, Gov. Stover and others made strong addresses; and closed just before the election with a series of three meetings at Las Vegas, Cerrillos, and Albuquerque, addressed by Gov. Prince on behalf of the Constitution; two of which by request of the Democratic committee were changed into joint discussions with Mr. Childers and Mr. Fergusson, respectively.

Major Jose D. Sena issued a manifesto in Spanish containing twenty-four reasons for Statehood.

CONSTITUTION OF 1890.

While the preponderance of work had been done in favor of adoption yet the result of the election was adverse by a large majority, the official vote being as follows:

Counties.	For.	Against.
Bernalillo	870	2,073
Colfax	234	651
Dona Ana	669	1,010
Grant	699	544
Lincoln	379	710
Mora	265	1,536
Rio Arriba	428	1,272
San Juan	87	182
San Miguel	790	3,211
Santa Fe	1,068	1,549
Sierra	227	717
Socorro	447	1,068
Taos	212	1,227
Valencia	1,118	430
Total	7,493	16,180

Majority against the Constitution 8,687.

The peculiar result was clearly and fairly explained in the official report of the Governor for 1891, which contains the following on the subject:

"At first sight this might appear to indicate a disinclination on the part of the people to assume the condition of statehood. This, however, is not the case. The circumstances were peculiar. The apportionment of delegates in the Constitutional Convention, as fixed by the legislative act which provided for the latter, was considered by the Democratic party leaders to be unjust to that party. They therefore refused to take any part in the election of delegates, and directed their party friends to abstain from voting. This order was quite generally followed, so that the convention itself, with a few notable exceptions, was solidly Republican. While this condition of things, by throwing the entire responsibility of the work on one party, no doubt caused the production of a more perfect instrument than would otherwise have been drafted, yet it alienated the bulk of the Democratic party and all of its official leaders from its support, and set the whole machinery of that party actively at work to bring about its defeat. Public speakers traversed the Territory in opposition, and easily excited prejudices among the large portion of the people who had never lived in a State, knew but little of the results of State government, and whose fears of the unknown were thus aroused against any change from the system with which they were familiar. All interests opposed to Statehood, or to any particular provision of the Constitution in question, worked behind the election machinery thus provided, and the result was as stated. It should be noted, however, that the political orators and party leaders most active in their opposition all repudiated the idea that they were opposed to Statehood itself, and asserted that their opposition was solely to the proposed Constitution and the method of its formation, and that on the main question they were as progressive as those they opposed."

The adverse vote had no effect on the efforts of the people for self-government, and all parties proceeded as before in endeavoring to secure admission through an Enabling Act of Congress.

The following extracts from the Constitution of 1889-90 are inserted here in order to show the progressive characteracter of that instrument, and also as suggestions of matters which should not be overlooked in future drafts of Constitutions:

ARTICLE II.

"Sec. 10. All lotteries or sale of lottery tickets are prohibited.

"Sec. 24. No officer, or person authorized by this Constitution to appoint any person to office, shall ever appoint to office any person who may be related to him by blood or marriage within the fourth degree of consanguinity according to the civil law rule of computation."

Sec. 25. The legislature shall pass liberal exemption laws; and there shall be exempt from levy and forced sale under any process from any court in this State, the parcel of ground and the buildings thereon, owned by the debtor and occupied by him as a residence, he being a householder and having a family, to the value of not less than twenty-five hundred dollars."

ARTICLE IV.

"Sec. 13. No member of the legislature shall, during the term for which he was elected, be appointed or elected to any civil office which has been created, or the emoluments thereof have been increased, during such term; nor receive any civil appointment to any office within the State."

"Sec. 18. No bill shall become a law except by a vote of a majority of all the members elected to each House, nor unless on its final passage the vote be taken by ayes and noes and the names of those voting entered on the journal."

"Sec. 22. The legislature shall not pass special or local laws on any of the following subjects:

(Here follows a list quite similar to that in the Constitution of 1872, but containing the following items).

"Claims or accounts against the State or any municipality;

"Refunding money paid into the treasury;

"Releasing persons from any debt or obligation to the State or any municipal or quasi-municipal corporation therein."

"Sec. 23. The legislature shall not grant to any corporation or to any person, any rights, privileges, immunities, or exemptions which shall not upon the same terms belong equally to all persons."

"Sec. 25. No bill for the appropriation of money, except for the ordinary expenses of the government, shall be introduced after the fiftieth day of the session except by unanimous consent."

ARTICLE V.

"Sec. 7. When any bill appropriating money from the public treasury shall have passed both Houses and been presented to the Governor, he shall have power to approve the same in whole or in part, and may return to the House in which it originated a copy of any part or parts of such bill which he may disapprove, with his objections thereto, when like proceedings shall be had as in the case of any bill returned by the Governor as a whole."

"Sec. 12. Neither the State treasurer nor auditor of public accounts shall hold office for two consecutive terms, nor shall either immediately succeed the other in office."

ARTICLE VII.

"Sec. 13. No person shall hold more than one lucrative office at the same time; but no appointment in the militia, nor the office of notary public, shall be considered a lucrative office."

ARTICLE IX.

"Sec. 1. Provision shall be made by law for the establishment and maintenance of a uniform system of public schools which shall be open to and sufficient for the education of all the children in the State, and shall be under the absolute control of the State, and free from sectarian or church control; and no other or different schools shall ever receive any aid or support from public funds. No sectarian tenet, creed or church doctrine shall be taught in the public schools."

ARTICLE XII.

"Sec. 4. No county, town, city or other municipal corporation shall ever become a stockholder in any joint stock company, corporation or association whatever, or raise money for, or make donations to or loan its credit to or in aid of, any such company, corporation or association."

"Sec. 11. No county seat shall be changed until a proposition designating the place to which the removal is proposed shall have been submitted to the electors of the county and received two-thirds of the vote cast by qualified electors."

ARTICLE XIII.

"Sec. 8. Any combination between individuals, associations or corporations having for its object, or which shall operate, to control the price of any article of manufacture or commerce, product of the soil or mine, is hereby prohibited and declared unlawful and against public policy; and the legislature shall provide such penalties and forfeitures as shall be sufficient to prevent all such unlawful combinations."

"Sec. 9. All railroad, transportation and express companies doing business in this State shall be common carriers, and all railroads owned or controlled by such companies shall be public highways, and the legislature shall pass laws to correct abuses and prevent unjust discrimination and extortion in the rates of freight, express and passenger tariffs on the different railroads, and in the charges of telephone, telegraphic and insurance companies in this State, and enforce such laws by adequate penalties, to the extent, if necessary for that purpose, of forfeiture of their property and franchise."

"Sec. 16. Any president or other officer of any banking institution, who shall receive or assent to the reception of deposits after he shall have knowledge that such banking institution is insolvent or in failing circumstances, shall be individually responsible for such deposits so received."

CHAPTER IX.

PROPOSED CHANGES OF NAME.

In other chapters we have had occasion to refer to various proposed changes in the name of New Mexico when it should enter the Union as a State, especially the attempt in the Omnibus Bill in the 50th Congress (1888) to call it Montezuma, and the peculiar provision in the bill introduced by Hon. Antonio Joseph, Feb. 15, 1889, which apparently sought to accomplish the same result by indirection. No such changes ever found favor in New Mexico, and the project was denounced as soon as known.

At a meeting of the people of New Mexico held in the court house, in the city of Santa Fe, in the winter of 1888-9, Hon. James A. Williamson presiding, a committee of 26, representing all portions of the Territory, was appointed on resolutions, with Judge Hazledine as its chairman. The committee reported the following, which were unanimously adopted:

"Whereas, the name of New Mexico has been for more than three hundred years applied to this Territory, and the inhabitants have for generations held that name in veneration and desire to perpetuate it in their history as the name of a sovereign State;

"Resolved, That simple justice to this people demands that they should be permitted to perpetuate the history and achievements of their forefathers by retaining "New Mexico" as the name of the new State."

These Resolutions were presented to the Senate April 7th, 1890, accompanied by a communication from Judge Hazledine.

Notwithstanding the strong sentiment in New Mexico against a change, from time to time various suggestions have continued to be made as to a new name for the future State, and some of these have been persistently advocated.

A favorite argument and one that might have weight if there was not so much sentiment and such a long historic association involved, is that the name New Mexico is confusing and that foreigners and even Americans from the east are likely to confound it with the Republic of Mexico. This has been illustrated by numerous anecdotes, which are often true, of apparently intelligent citizens of New York or Massachusetts who direct letters to Mexico instead of New Mexico, or express surprise that Albuquerque is in the United States or that they see an American flag in Santa Fe or that American postage stamps are good in Las Vegas; and it is said that the old name is an obstacle to immigrtion and will handicap the progress of the new State.

One of the most persistent efforts in this direction was to establish a State of Lincoln, especially since Washington was similarly honored in the far northwest. This was earnestly advocated as far back as the "60s" and even within the last few months a number of communications have appeared in the press in favor of its adoption.

David Dudley Field for some reason felt a great interest in the subject of the name and wrote a number of letters to periodicals some twenty years ago earnestly advocating the name of Montezuma; and he even went to the trouble of visiting Washington and interviewing prominent members of Congress in behalf of this project. The peculiar provision in section 20 of the Omnibus Bill of 1888 was probably inserted owing to his solicitation and influence.

More recently, Hon. B. S. Rodey, one of the most enthusiastic of Statehood workers, has argued strongly in favor of the adoption of Acoma as the name of the new State, possibly in order that alphabetically it should lead in the roll at National Conventions and similar meetings.

This fact is that New Mexico is altogether the most historic and dignified name in the United States. There is but one geographical name in the entire country older than this, and that is the name of Florida. Long before the settlement of Jamestown, still longer before the Hollanders came to New Amsterdam or the Pilgrims landed at Plymouth, the name of New Mexico had been fixed and established, and was known throughout the civilized world. It dates back to 1583, more than three and a quarter centuries ago. In that year Espejo marched up the Rio Grande in hopes of rescuing from a martyr's fate the three Franciscan missionaries who had settled upon its banks near the modern Bernalillo.

After passing the desert to the south, he came into the beautiful and fertile valley of the Great River of the North, and was so struck with its resemblance to some of the most charming spots in New Spain that he christened it "New Mexico." There is no doubt of this fact or of its date; they do not rest on rumor or tradition.

So important was the discovery considered and so much interest did it create in the City of Mexico, that the Rev. Padre Juan Gonzales de Mendoza, visiting that city on his return from his travels in China, incorporated the entire history of Espejo's expedition into his book on "The Great Kingdom of China;" and as such it was not only published immediately in Spain, but translated into French, Italian and English, and thus made known to all Europe. A copy of the French edition, published in Paris in 1588, is among the literary treasures of the New Mexico Historical Society in the Palace at Santa Fe. It contains the full narration of the chivalrous expedition of Espejo from the day that it left Santa Barbara in New Biscay until its return. And here we have a chapter headed "Of New Mexico and how it was discovered," which proceeds to tell that in the year 1583 Antonio de Espejo, after traveling up the Rio del Norte, discovered a land of fifteen provinces which he called New Mexico. Thus the antiquity of the name is absolutely established; and from then until now, through all these years of time, that name has never changed.

And as to the dignity which that name represents; New Mexico was never an ordinary province of New Spain, like the regions to the south of it. It was always a separate government, with authorities appointed directly by the Spanish king, and in all ancient documents it was called "The Kingdom of New Mexico." This high dignity it possessed from the very beginning. The oldest document issued in New Mexico, of which we have any knowledge, was written before the Spanish settlement of Santa Fe, at

San Gabriel, the first capital of the province, situated where Chamita station now stands, in the wide valley at the junction of the Rio Grande and the Chama. It is signed by the first Governor and Captain General, Don Juan de Onate, under date of October, 1603. This venerable document describes Onate as Governor, Adelantado and Pacificator of "The Kingdom and Provinces of New Mexico."

An examination of any of the ancient Spanish documents fortunately preserved to New Mexico by the Historical Society, as well as those in the Archives now in Washington, of which the Territory is deprived until she has the power of Statehood by which to reclaim them, will prove that this dignified and exalted title was constantly applied to New Mexico. They will be found to be dated in this language: "Done in the City of Santa Fe, Capital of the Kingdom and Provinces of New Mexico;" and the title of the ruler was uniformly "Governor and Captain General of this Kingdom and Provinces of New Mexico." Everywhere the word is "reino," kingdom; and there is no other part of the United States that ever possessed so exalted a title.

In its extent as well as in its title New Mexico excelled in dignity and grandeur. By consulting any of the ancient maps in the Historical Society's rooms it will be seen that for more than a century the whole range of country now constituting the southern part of the United States, from the Pacific to the Atlantic, was divided between New Mexico and Florida; the dividing line being the Mississippi river. Then for another hundred years there were three divisions instead of two:—Louisiana occupying the Mississippi valley in the center; but the northern boundary of New Mexico running up indefinitely to the arctic regions.

So the people are naturally proud of the historic name. For three hundred and twenty-five years this great region had been known as New Mexico. It is true that in later years it has lost part of its area. Arizona, with parts of Nevada and Utah, have been taken off on the west. Southern Colorado was cut off to enlarge that sister State. Texas occupies much of its old eastern territory. But still, through all the ages, under varying forms of government; under three different nationalities; sometimes a kingdom, sometimes a province, sometimes a territory; through revolutionis and re-conquests and restorations, New Mexico had progressed under its original proper name unchanged and it was hoped unchangable.

It is a fact not generally known, that down to a few days before the final report of the Senate Substitute for the Hamilton Statehood Bill, in 1910, there was a strong inclination in very influential quarters to change the name of New Mexico in the bill to something modern, and this was only averted by the positive assurances from representatives of the Territory that any such change would meet such strong opposition from the people of New Mexico as to place the Statehood proposition in grave danger of rejection.

The only official endorsement of a change, was in the passage of the Joint Statehood Bill of 1906, giving the consolidated State the name of Arizona. The fact is, that the people of the Territory at large, especially the descendants of the original Spanish settlers and the older residents among the English speaking population, have never looked on any change with favor; and the day will be far distant, if it ever arrives, when the people of the present Territory will consent to a change which will break their historic connection with the past and blot from the map a name which has remained there continuously for over three hundred years.

CHAPTER X.

FAVORABLE INFLUENCES.

Throughout the long duration of the "Struggle" events have occurred, and influences have been exerted, which have aided materially in the ultimate success of the Statehood movement, and which deserve recognition here. Such are the planks in the national platforms of the great political parties; the action of State and Territorial Conventions on the subject; the formal hearings before the committees of the Senate and House of Representatives; the written statements made to those committees; articles contributed to leading journals in defense of New Mexico and advocacy of Statehood; and resolutions passed and addresses made on the subject in important national bodies of large influence.

Some of the more important of these will be referred to in separate chapters, under their appropriate heads, and others are grouped together here; but all shoold be considered in connection with the more systematic narrative of events in the record of Congressional action.

ARTICLES IN PERIODICALS.

During a long period, articles have been sent to journals of large influence, by ardent friends of the cause, and have had their influence on public opinion.

The first of these after the dozen years of inaction, was contributed by Hon. L. B. Prince to the New York Tribune under date of January 10, 1889, with the title "Admission of New Mexico; both justice and expediency demand it." This was in part an answer to a scurrilous article in the Chicago Tribune, and an argument for immediate admission. It was followed up by similar articles in the New York Mail and Express on January 16th, 1889, and the Indianapolis Journal on January 20th, 1889. Somewhat later he was invited by the editor of the North American Review to contribute an article on the subject to that periodical, which gave an opportunity of presenting the facts to the most cultivated constituency in the country.

On December 9th, 1893, Judge A. L. Morrison sent an excellent and effective article to the Chicago Inter-Ocean, defending the people of New Mexico from the strictures contained in an editorial in that journal a few days before.

On January 4, 1900, Col. R. E. Twitchell wrote a vigorous and characteristic article to the St. Louis Globe-Democrat, entitled "Progress of New Mexico; some figures that serve to correct false impressions." As introduction he said: "The Territory of New Mexico has been the most maligned, the least appreciated and the most poorly understood portion of Uncle Sam's domain." "If there is one thing above another that the ordinary dweller in the lands east of the Mississippi can thoroughly understand, it is figures. Your true-blue Yankee has a mania for figures and statistics. One of the first things a Bostonese infant has impressed upon him is the fact that figures don't lie." And then he proceeded with some most convincing statistics.

During his prolonged service in Washington, Hon. B. S. Rodey wrote numerous letters to the eastern press, correcting misstatements and appealing for justice to New Mexico in no uncertain tones and in his emphatic and unmistakable language; and these undoubtedly had an excellent effect in educating public opinion in that section of the country.

On January 6th, 1903, Gov. Prince wrote another letter to the New York Tribune, which was afterwards printed in pamphlet form and widely distributed to members of Congress and others, entitled "The Claims of New Mexico."

Many other patriotic citizens have aided in this work of publicity, with good results; though the general ignorance of the country as to the resources and conditions of the southwest seems so dense that it is difficult to dispel. It is not many years since a leading journal of national influences spoke of "four-fifths of the people" of New Mexico being "Peon Aztec Indians," whatever they may be!

STATEHOOD CONVENTIONS.

A Statehood Convention was called by Gov. Otero to express the sentiment of the people relative to the admission of New Mexico to the Union, and met at Albuquerque on October 15th and 16th, 1901. Among other notable speeches, was one by Gov. Murphy of Arizona. The convention passed strong resolutions, which were reported by a committee headed by L. C. Grove of San Juan County, embodying not only arguments and statements of facts, but declarations of principles in clear and convincing terms. They are drawn in the general style of the Declaration of Independence and contain an arraignment of Congress similar to that of King George the Third in the Declaration.

After a suitable preamble they "solemnly publish and declare that New Mexico of right ought to be a free and independent State," and they close with the following sentences:

"WHEREFORE, Having endured all these things, through all these years, supported the flag and the Constitution in two wars, we most respectfully appeal to the sense of justice and righteousness of the Congress, and

PRAY: That it will not permit a government of our people, for our people and by our people to perish from our hopes, but that under God it will grant us a new lease of freedom by granting us STATEHOOD."

Another Statehood Convention, called by Gov. Curry, met in the Capitol at Santa Fe, on November 30th, 1907, and was largely attended from various sections of the Territory by representative citizens. The governor, secretary and judges of the Supreme Court, occupied the platform. Hon, T. B. Catron delivered an address of welcome, and the convention temporarily organized with Gov. Curry as president, and Hon. J. M. Hervey and Hon. R. L. Baca as secretaries. Subsequently Hon. W. S. Hopewell was made permanent president.

Gov. Curry announced good tidings from Washington, where he had recently seen the President and various prominent men and had received gratifying and encouraging assurances. Hon. L. B. Prince presented the latest Trans-Mississippi resolutions and told of the enthusiasm that he had just witnessed in Oklahoma over their acquired Statehood. Judge Morrison counseled harmony and careful avoidance of partisanship. A number of brief addresses were made, and resolutions urging immediate action on the Statehood Bill were passed and directed to be sent to Washington.

WESTERN CONGRESSES.

Public sentiment throughout the whole of the Great West has been strongly in favor of the admission of New Mexico from the beginning, and every proper opportunity has been taken advantage of to make this manifest in the way of resolutions passed by important representative bodies. The most widely known and influential of these is the Trans-Mississippi Commercial Congress, and beginning in 1892 at New Orleans, that great organization has given at each of its annual sessions, expression to its belief and its wishes on this subject.

Hon. L. Bradford Prince was for many years the representative of New Mexico in that Congress, of which he was president in 1892 and presiding vice-president at three other sessions, and he regularly presented the resolutions, which were always unanimously adopted. This included the Congresses at New Orleans, Ogden, San Francisco, St. Louis, Omaha, Salt Lake, Wichita, Houston, and Cripple Creek, as well as more recent ones. Usually a brief statement was all that was required to insure this result, but at Omaha in 1895, and at Cripple Creek in July, 1901, he made addresses of considerable length which were published in pamphlet form and aided in creating a correct public sentiment.

The National Irrigation Congress has always carefully refrained from passing any resolution not directly connected with irrigation and related subjects; but at the session held in Colorado Springs in 1892 it made an exception to this rule and on motion of Hon. G. A. Richardson of New Mexico, after an enthusiastic speech from Hon.

John Henry Smith of Utah, passed a resolution in favor of New Mexican Statehood.

Many other western organizations have followed the lead of these representative bodies and added the weight of their influence in favor of justice to New Mexico; and to all of these the thanks of her people are due.

CHAPTER XI.

NATIONAL CONVENTIONS.

In this connection it would be improper to omit mention of the various planks in the platforms of the leading parties of the country as adopted in their National Conventions in presidential years; although their wording has usually been so careful and almost indefinite that their spirit might be violated without actually contradicting their letter.

In 1888 the Republican National Convention at Chicago, which was earnestly requested to recommend Statehood, passed the following resolution on that subject, which although excellent is rather general in the language employed:

"The government by Congress of the Territories is based upon necessity only, to the end that they may become States in the Union; therefore, whenever the conditions of population, material resources, public intelligence, and morality, are such as to insure a stable local government therein, the people of such Territories should be permitted, as a right inherent in them, to form for themselves constitutions and State governments and be admitted into the Union."

The Democraic National Convention at St. Louis in the same year took much stronger ground and mentioned New Mexico by name. It is to be remembered in considering these resolutions that at that time and until 1896 Utah was still a Territory and there was so much popular antagonism to the admission of that Territory that both parties handled the subject with considerable care. The following is the democratic plank:

"Resolved, That a just and liberal policy should be pursued in reference to the Territories; that the right of self government is inherent in the people and guaranteed under the Constitution; that the Territories of Washington, Dakota, Montana and New Mexico are, by virtue of population and development, entitled to admission into the

Union of States; and we unqualifiedly condemn the course of the republican party in refusing Statehood and self government to their people."

In 1892 the National Republican Convention gave very meagre space to its plank on this subject. The following is the resolution:

"We favor the admission of the remaining Territories at the earliest practicable day, having due regard to the interests of the people of the Territories and the United States."

The democratic convention at Chicago in the same year was rather more outspoken in its statement, as it had been four years before. Its plank was as follows:

"We approve the action of the present House of Representatives in passing bills for the admission into the Union as States of the Territories of New Mexico and Arizona, and we favor the early admission of all the Territories having necessary population and resources to admit them to Statehood."

Four years after, in 1896, the republican national convention again passed a resolution on the subject, but did not vary in a single word from the language of the resolution which was passed in 1892.

The democratic national convention at Chicago also followed very nearly the language which it employed four years before, but it added Oklahoma to the list of Territories specifically mentioned, the plank in their platform being as follows:

'We favor the admission of the Territories of New Mexico, Arizona and Oklahoma into the Union as states, and we favor the early admission of all the Territories having the necessary population and resources to entitle them to Statehood."

In 1900 the Republican National Convention at Philadelphia made its plank on Statehood even shorter than before but very much more distinct. The resolution reads as follows:

"We favor home rule for, and the early admission to Statehood of, the Territories of New Mexico, Arizona and Oklahoma."

The Democratic Convention at Kansas City made the most political capital possible out of the situation and in its promise went further than the republicans by the use of the important word "immediate." The plank in the National platform reads as follows:

"We denounce the failure of the republican party to carry out its pledges to grant Statehood to the Territories of Arizona, New Mexico and Oklahoma. We promise the people of those Territories immediate Statehood, and home rule during their condition as Territories."

In 1904 the Republican National Convention, which met in Chicago, added nothing to its previous declarations.

The Democratic National Convention, at St. Louis, added to its former statement a declaration in favor of separate Statehood for New Mexico and Arizona, as Joint Statehood had become somewhat of an issue. The Statehood plank in its platform is as follows:

"We favor the admission of the Territory of Oklahoma and the Indian Territory. We also favor the immediate admission of Arizona and New Mexico, as separate States."

Finally we come to 1908.

The Democratic National Convention at Denver reiterated its former declarations and pledges in amplified form. The platform says:

"The National Democratic party has for the last sixteen years labored for the admission of Arizona and New Mexico, as separate States of the Federal Union, and recognizing that each possesses every qualification to successfully maintain separate State governments, we favor the immediate admission of these Territories as separate States."

The Republican National Convention, again meeting in Chicago, preserved its characteristic brevity of expression, but, in the two lines of its declaration, for the first time gave an unequivocal pledge in favor not only of separate Statehood, but of immediate admission. This concession by eastern republicans was not obtained without a long and vigorous struggle by the delegates from New Mexico and their friends. The credit for final success, by the insertion of the word "immediate," is due to Hon. H. O. Bursum, chairman of the Territorial Republican Committee, through whose tact and pertinacity it was achieved.

While the exact wording of political platforms is not always of great importance, and too often the platforms themselves are regarded as more for campaign use than an inviolable pledge of official action; yet in this case the clear and distinct declaration of the resolution has been of the highest value. Its very brevity added to its force. President Taft has taken the highest ground as to the obligation of a party and its official representatives to carry into effect the pledges of its declaration of principles. Finding in the Chicago platform this unequivocal statement regarding "immediate admission," he insisted that a Republican Congress was bound to carry it into effect. Without this conscientious construction of party honor and party duty, on the part of the President, it is more than doubtful whether the Statehood Bill of 1910 would have been passed. Without this clear-cut plank, he would not have felt obliged to insist on its fulfilment; so that while so many platform declarations above recorded have been without effect, the very important influence of the last one adds new dignity and respect to the solemnly adopted pledges of great parties.

CHAPTER XII.

HEARINGS IN WASHINGTON.

Since the revival of interest in Statehood about twenty years ago, and during the consideration of the constant succession of bills of various kinds relating to admission to the Union, by the Committees on Territories of the House and the Senate, there have been a number of hearings on the subject, many of them of importance, the printed reports of which shed much light on the progress of the struggle and the changing aspects in which the subject has been presented.

It is not necessary to enumerate all of these, but the principal ones, which led to results or influenced public opinion, will be briefly referred to.

1890.

The first of these was on May 5, 1890, before the Senate Committee on Territories, of which Senator O. H. Platt of Connecticut was then chairman. The committee was the one of fifty-four members appointed by the Governor at the formal request of the Bureau of Immigration, to visit Washington, principally in relation to a land court, to school lands and to irrigation. It was entirely a voluntary matter of patriotic service, each member paying his own expenses, and their character is shown by the fact that no less than twenty-nine—more than half the entire delegation appointed,—actually went to Washington, and remained there engaged in the work of their mission for nearly a month. It was undoubtedly the strongest delegation which ever visited Washington from New Mexico and the most successful in the accomplishment of results. The passage of the Act creating the Court of Private Land Claims, which settled the titles to the land grants in the Territory, was the most immediate result of its labors. It visited the President, every member of the Cabinet, the Assistant Secretary of the Treasury, the Commissioner and Deputy Commissioner of the Land Office and the Mexican minister; and was afforded hearings by the Senate

HEARINGS IN WASHINGTON. 75

Committees on Territories, Public Lands and Private Land Claims, and by the House Committees on Territories, Education, Private Land Claims, and Irrigation. The reasons which induced the committee to take up the matter of Statehood appears in the proceedings hereafter mentioned.

The names of the twenty-nine actually present in Washington were as follows:

Hon. L. Bradford Prince, Governor.
Hon. Trinidad Alarid, Territorial Auditor.
Hon. S. B. Axtell, ex-Governor and ex-Chief Justice.
A. J. Bahney, P. M., Socorro.
Ira M. Bond, Editor, Albuquerque.
S. E. Booth, Chairman County Commissioners, San Miguel County.
George H. Cross, News Edttor, New Mexican.
C. H. Gildersleeve, Santa Fe.
S. L. Hauck, San Pedro.
Hon. W. C. Hazledine, Genl. Solicitor A. & P. R. R.
W. H. Kennedy, Cerrillos.
J. C. Lea, Roswell.
Col. W. G. Marmon, Laguna.
Hon. T. B. Mills, Las Vegas.
J. S. Raynolds, Pres. 1st Nat. Bank, Albuquerque.
Frank W. Smith, Las Cruces.
E. W. Spencer, Albuquerque.
Hon. E. S. Stover, Albuquerque.
A. Staab, Santa Fe.
Hon. L. S. Trimble, Ex-M. C., Albuquerque.
George H. Utter, Silver City.
John P. Victory, Santa Fe.
Gen. J. A. Williamson, Pres. A. & P. R. R.
W. C. Wrigley, Dist. Atty., Raton.
Levi A. Hughes, Int. Revenue Collector.
J. B. Bowman, Las Cruces.
George F. Patrick, Silver City.
Hon. Thomas Smith, ex-U. S. Attorney.

At the hearing, Gov. Prince opened the discussion, as follows:

Mr. Chairman:—I would like to call attention to the size and character of the delegation present this morning. It is not the ordinary kind of delegation coming of its own volition to ask for legislation to secure personal interests, but it is a regularly commissioned delegation, appointed at the instance of the Bureau of Immigration of New Mexico to come to Washington to secure, if possible, certain legislation looking to the material development of that country.

When they arrived here they found that the subjects as to which they had been sent, apparently cannot be obtained without Statehood. Some of them naturally follow admission to the Union, and others it seems practically impossible to attain until we have representation in both Houses of Congress. So that this committee, which came here to attend to these matters relating to the material prosperity of the Territory, has been forced to the conclusion unanimously that that prosperity cannot be attained without Statehood. We therefore come before you today, Democrats and Republicans, representing all parts of the Territory and every interest in it, unanimously to ask for Statehood for New Mexico.

After presenting the claims of the Territory quite fully, the discussion was continued by Hon. E. S. Stover, Ira M. Bond, George F. Patrick, Hon. L. S. Trimble, George H. Utter, Col. Thomas Smith, Hon. J. P. Victory and Hon. Antonio Joseph; the Senators taking an active part being the chairman and Senators Cullum, Stewart, Payne, and Manderson.

This same committee of twenty-nine also had a hearing before the House Committee on Territories, which courteously held a special session for the purpose, on April 30th, 1890. A somewhat similar presentation of the claims of New Mexico was made by Gov. Prince, Judge Trimble and Judge Axtell, and numerous questions by members of the committee, including Mr. Springer of Illinois, Mr. Dorsey of Nebraska, and others, were satisfactorily answered.

HEARINGS IN WASHINGTON. 77

1902.

House Bill No. 12543, providing for the admission of Arizona, New Mexico and Oklahoma to Statehood, having been referred to the Senate Committee on Territories, that committee gave a hearing to the delegates of those Territories and such parties as they might present, on June 28th and 30th, 1902.

This was immediately subsequent to the passage in the Senate of the resolution empowering the committee to visit the Territories for the purpose of investigating conditions there.

Of the Senate Committee there were present Senators Beveridge, (Chairman), Bard, Bate, Dillingham, Heitfeld, and Keene.

The first statement received was that of Hon. Marcus A. Smith, delegate from Arizona, presenting the claims of that Territory, and laying stress on the injustice done as to population, by the census of 1900.

Hon. Bernard S. Rodey, delegate from New Mexico, followed, on behalf of that Territory, and made a very strong and comprehensive statement regarding its history, population, resources, finances, and the general character of the people. The members of the committee asked a multitude of questions, largely as to the courts, schools and language.

He was followed by Maj. W. H. H. Llewellyn, of Las Cruces, who made a forcible plea for Statehood and gave valuable testimony as to the valley of the Rio Grande, the prospects of irrigation, public education, the desire for Statehood and other appropriate matters.

John L. Gay of the Railway Mail Service was then examined, and was succeeded by Ira M. Bond, the well known editor and correspondent, who gave the result of many years of experience in New Mexico, as to the people, their good citizenship, loyalty and various characteristics.

A. F. Codington then spoke of the universal desire for Statehood, and Mr. Rodey closed the hearing so far as New Mexico was concerned by a statement as to irrigation and water rights. During the entire hearing, the members of the committee displayed much interest and occupied a large proportion of the time by questions.

1903.

In December, 1903, Delegate Rodey's Bill for the admission of New Mexico being before the committee, the Delegate arranged for a hearing before the Committee on Territories of the House, with special reference to disparaging statements that had appeared in the recent report of the Senate Committee made by Senator Beveridge.

The hearing commenced on Dec. 11th and was continued on December 15th, 17th and 18th, Hon. Edward L. Hamilton presiding and twelve other members of the committee being present. The discussion was opened by Hon. G. A. Richardson of Roswell in an able address, and he was followed by Hon. L. B. Prince, Mayor Ishmael Sparks of Santa Fe, and Hon. B. S. Rodey then delegate from New Mexico. The arguments of the New Mexicans were mostly on the general principles involved in the claim for self government, and the questions of the committee were mainly directed to the condition of the native population. The members of the committee taking the most active part in the discussion were the Chairman and Messrs. Lloyd, Powers, Robinson, Spalding, Sterling, Capron and Wilson.

1906.

In January, 1906, the Joint Statehood Bill for New Mexico and Arizona being before the House Committee on Territories, a protracted hearing was held which extended continuously from January 16th to January 20th, inclusive, the report of which occupied 190 pages. Hon. Edward L. Hamilton, the chairman, presided, with twelve others of the committee present.

There was a very large delegation in attendance from Arizona, all of whom were opposed to Joint Statehood, and presented arguments and facts bearing on that issue. Mr. Dwight B. Heard was chairman of the delegation and opened the discussion after an introduction by ex-Delegate Smith. He was followed by Eugene B. O'Neill, R. E. Morrison, Gov. N. O. Murphy, W. S. Sturgis, Gen. A. J. Sampson, Dr. A. J. Chandler, Rev. H. M. Shields, B. A.

Fowler, A. J. Doran, Roy S. Goodrich, E. S. Campbell, J. J. Riggs, and George French of Arizona; and Senator W. A. Clark of Montana, also spoke on the subject of taxation of mines in Arizona. Hon. W. H. Andrews spoke briefly and Hon. B. S. Rodey at considerable length in support of the project for Joint Statehood. Extracts from some of the speeches of the Arizona delegates have been reproduced herein in connection with the strong feeling in that Territory against Joint Statehood with New Mexico.

1908.

In January, 1908, immediate action on the Statehood Bill introduced by Delegate Andrews had been promised, and to facilitate it, Gov. Curry of New Mexico proceeded to Washington and arrangements were made for a hearing before the House Committee on Territories.

This hearing was held on January 29th and was opened by an address by Hon. L. B. Prince, who presented the Resolutions of the Trans-Mississippi Congress passed unanimously at its session at Muskogee in November, 1907, strongly endorsing immediate Statehood for New Mexico. He then proceeded to present the usual arguments for admission, based on the right to self government, on population, wealth, fairness, etc., but laying particular stress on the vicious and un-American character of a provincial form of government. He was followed by Gov. Curry, who invited the committee, in case it did not take immediate action, to visit New Mexico and examine the conditions for themselves. Hon. W. H. Andrews, the Congressional Delegate, closed the session with an appeal for favorable action. The members of the committee evincing special interest by taking part in the discusion were the chairman and Messrs. Houston, Davenport, Higgins, etc.

1910.

The last important hearing was that held in February, 1910, before the Senate Committee on Territories in the hope of inducing an early report on the House Committee bill, generally called the "Hamilton Bill," for the admission of New Mexico and Arizona as separate States, which had passed the House and was then in the Senate Committee. At this hearing, which extended over three days, the 18th, 19th and 20th, both Territories were represented. The special subjects that were discussed outside of the general issues, were the payment of certain county bonds validated by Act of Congress, and a provision of the Arizona election law of March 10th, 1909, which practically disfranchised a large class of citizens.

Senator Beveridge presided and Senators Dillingham, Burnham, Kean, Piles, Frazier, Hughes, Dick, and Owen were present.

Those taking part in the discussion for New Mexico were Hon. L. B. Prince, Hon. C. A. Spiess, and Hon. N. B. Laughlin; Mr. L. A. Hughes also being present; and from Arizona, Hon. Mark Smith, Hon. Ralph H. Cameron, Robert E. Morrison and J. L. Hubbell; and also Hon. Bird S. Coler of Brooklyn, and Rev. W. H. Ketchem of Washington. In the New Mexico hearing, which occupied the 18th of February, besides the discussion of the bonds, Gov. Prince laid special stress on the previous experience of the people of New Mexico in framing constitutions of great excellence, and exhibited copies of the Constitution of 1850 and that of 1890 to the committee. All of the speakers, in answer to Senator Beveridge, assured him that they approved the strict provisions of the proposed law as to the disposition of the public land.

The report of the bill, and its final passage and enactment into law, followed closely on this hearing.

CHAPTER XIII.

STATEMtNTS TO COMMITTEES.

From time to time carefully prepared statements have been submitted to Congressional Committees, which embodied facts and arguments systematically arranged.

Such was the document presented to the Senate Committee by Hon. W. C. Hazledine, accompanying the Constitution of 1890.

Such was the argument submitted to the House Committee, in 1902, by Dr. Nathan E. Boyd, relative to the value of Statehood in connection with the protection of material rights concerning agriculture and irrigation.

In 1892, the Statehood question had become very prominent, and was occupying much public attention. To meet the demand for accurate information and refute oft repeated calumnies, Gov. Prince was called upon to make a statement which should cover all the points involved. This was done in a letter to the Senate Committee on Territories; and this letter, afterwards embodied in the Governor's annual report for 1892, was the first systematic document published on the subject and became the foundation of a host of articles and speeches for many years. As it embodies, as briefly as possible, the whole argument for New Mexican Statehood, it is inserted here in full, although some of the statistics have been superseded by those more recent.

Executive Office,
Santa Fe, June 25, 1892.

HON. H. O. PLATT,

Chairman Committee on Territories, United States Senate:

On June 6, 1892, House Bill No. 7136, being "An act to enable the people of New Mexico to form a constitution and State government," passed the House of Representatives, and on being received in the Senate was referred to your committee.

This is a matter of the most vital importance to the people of this Territory, and I therefore take the liberty of addressing you on the subject and submitting some of the considerations which seem to me to render a longer continuance of territorial government in New Mexico improper and in violation of the rights of our people as American citizens.

RIGHT OF SELF-GOVERNMENT.

Self-government is an inherent right of American citizenship; in fact it is inseparable from the fundamental principles of republican institutions. The right to a representative voice in the legislative body which enacts the laws which he is to obey and imposes the taxes which he is obliged to pay is one dear to every American, and the right to take part in the selection of the national Chief Magistrate and of the local governor and similar officials is likewise one of which he will not willingly be deprived.

These principles of self-government are so fundamental in our institutions that no citizen should be deprived of the right except under such peculiar circumstances as render its exercise impossible or dangerous.

To apply this practically, while in a section of country the people are so few or so poor as to make self-government impossible, they can be temporarily organized under a territorial government, in order to protect life and property; but the moment they are able to become self-governing they are entitled to that right.

No circumstance now exists in relation to the people of New Mexico which justifies their being longer deprived of their full rights under a State government. If one of them moves into Colorado or into Texas, he is immediately invested with the full rights of American citizenship; if he moves back, he loses them. This is improper and absurd. He is no more intelligent or honest or patriotic because he has crossed an imaginary line, nor does he lose any good qualities when he recrosses it.

Lack of sufficient numbers, or property, or intelligence might cause from necessity a temporary suspension of full civil rights to the inhabitants of a district of country, but I will endeavor to show, briefly but plainly, that neither of such conditions exists in New Mexico at present.

SPECIAL OBLIGATIONS.

Apart from the obligation which the nation owes to each of its citizens to secure to him the right of self-government, except where special exigencies prevent, specific promises were made to the people of New Mexico at the time of its acquisition, which have hitherto been disregarded. When Gen. Kearny made his peaceful entry into Santa Fe, he issued a formal proclamation on August 22, 1846, assuming the government of the entire Territory, and containing this statement: "It is the wish and intention of the United States to provide for New Mexico a free government, with the least possible delay, similar to those in the United States." The people were satisfied with the pacific sentiments of the American commander, relied on the promises of the proclamation, and offered no opposition to the occupation of the whole area of New Mexico. The treaty of Guadalupe Hidalgo, executed February 21, 1848, confirmed this promise.

ATTEMPTS TO OBTAIN STATEHOOD.

Relying on these pledges and anxious to possess all the rights of American citizenship, the people, early in 1850, held a convention, adopted a constitution, elected State officers, a legislature, and William S. Messervy as member of Congress. In July the legislature elected R. H. Weightman and F. C. Cunningham as Senators, and they, with the member of Congress, proceeded to Washington. While on the journey they were met by the intelligence of the passage, on September 9, of the famous "compromise measure," which admitted California as a State and relegated New Mexico to the condition of a territory.

From that time to the present, attempts to secure admission have constantly been made. The Territorial legislature has repeatedly memorialized Congress on the subject, the delegates have introduced enabling acts, and the people have never rested contentedly under their deprivation of the rights of citizenship. Congress has not entirely failed to respond to these appeals. Both Houses of the Forty-third Congress passed an enabling act, the House by a vote of 160 to 54 and the Senate by 32 to 11. The bill was slightly amended in the Senate and failed because it was impossible at the end of the session (it passed the Senate February 24) to bring it up for concurrence in the House. If it was proper to admit New Mexico in 1874, before it possessed a mile of railroad, a single public building, a developed mine, a matured orchard, or an alfalfa field, what reason can now be given for delay, when its population has greatly increased, its condition vastly improved, and its resources of all kinds are being developed into sources of wealth?

POPULATION.

In this respect the claim to statehood is indisputable. No Territory at the time of its admission, with the exception of Dakota, has contained the population now in New Mexico. By the census of 1890 it had 153,076 inhabitants, without counting the Indians on the reservations. The real population, as has been conclusively shown in public documents and is practically unquestioned, was between 180,000 and 185,000, the difficulty of full enumeration where the area is so vast and the population so scattered accounting for the difference. But, taking the census figures, the above statement as to other Territories is correct. The following table shows the date of the admission of each Territory, with its population according to the next preceding census. Of course, in some cases, there had been considerable growth between the census and the date of admission, but there is likewise an increase in New Mexico since 1890.

STATEMENTS TO COMMITTEES.

State.	Date of admission.	Population.	State.	Date of admission.	Population.
Tennessee	1796	35,691	California	1850	92,597
Ohio	1802	48,365	Minnesota	1858	6,077
Louisiana	1812	76,556	Oregon	1859	13,294
Indiana	1816	24,530	Kansas	1861	107,206
Mississippi	1817	*40,353	Nevada	1864	6,857
Illinois	1818	12,282	Nebraska	1867	28,841
Alabama	1819	(†)	Colorado	1876	39,864
Missouri	1821	66,557	North Dakota	1889	‡328,808
Arkansas	1836	30,388	South Dakota	1889	‡182,919
Michigan	1837	31,639	Washington	1889	75,116
Florida	1845	54,477	Montana	1889	39,159
Iowa	1846	43,112	Idaho	1890	84,385
Wisconsin	1848	30,945	Wyoming	1890	60,705

* Including Alabama.
† Included with Mississippi.
‡ By census of 1890. The population of both Dakotas in 1880 was 135,177.

The lesson drawn from this table becomes more marked when we remember that in many of the Territories mentioned a large fraction of the population was made up of slaves who were not citizens and had no vote, and further that in nearly all of them the proportion of aliens was far greater than in New Mexico. Thus, in Missouri there were over 10,000 slaves; in Florida, over 25,000, and in Louisiana over 34,000. When these numbers are deducted, it reduces the self-governing population quite materially.

So it is evident that there is now no reason, on the score of lack of sufficient population, for depriving the people of New Mexico of the ordinary rights of citizens. On the contrary it has more population than Idaho and Wyoming combined, considerably more than Montana, nearly or quite four times as much as Nevada and really 15,000 more than Delaware.

FINANCIAL STRENGTH.

The next question is whether the value of taxable property is sufficient to support a State government. If not, that might be a valid reason for longer delay. But we find that the assessed valuation of property in 1891 was $45,329,563. This is much larger than that of many other Territories at the time of their admission. The valuation of the last two States, for example, was as follows: Idaho, $28,000,000; Wyoming $31,000,000. The credit of New

Mexico is excellent, notwithstanding the prejudice against Territorial securities in the financial centers. The only bonds issued during the last four years were $25,000 for the completion of the insane asylum, and although there was some question as to their being in excess of the limit established by Congress, yet they sold for 105½. Since July, 1889, the Territory has been gradually redeeming and canceling its outstanding penitentiary bonds, to an amount between $40,000 and $50,000. These were bought at the lowest offers, after thorough advertising, and yet we have been compelled to pay from 107 to 117 per cent for them.

RESOURCES.

The resources of the Territory, as the foundation of its ability to sustain its own government permanently, are properly a matter for inquiry. And on this subject we may make the broad assertion that New Mexico is endowed with greater natural resources, and in greater variety, than any other State or Territory of the Union. This probably sounds extravagant, and may be considered as a specimen of western hyperbole, but while it is a bold statement, it is made with an entire appreciation of its full significance, and is well considered and deliberate. Only one approaches it, and that is California; and the possession of almost limitless beds of coal, both bituminous and anthracite, give New Mexico a superiority even over that favored State.

PUBLIC PROPERTY.

No Territory has ever erected so many public buildings, or possessed so much public property as New Mexico. Without the slightest aid from the National Government, it has built a most beautiful capitol, a substantial penitentiary, and more recently an insane asylum, university, agricultural college and school of mines. All these latter structures are more than creditable, they are sources of pride and gratification; and they are paid for from taxation without the incurring of any indebtedness, except the sum of $25,000 to complete the insane asylum. In nearly every western State the institutions of a similar character have been erected wholly or in part by grants of land made at the time of their admission, but New Mexico has not waited for such assistance. In addition to the above, more than half of our counties have erected commodious and elegant court houses of stone or brick within the past ten years.

It seems strange that with all these facts in her favor, New Mexico should have been so long deprived of statehood. It would be foolish to ignore the fact that there has existed in the eastern mind a prejudice against her on account of the supposed

CHARACTER OF THE POPULATION.

By many the people are looked upon as foreign and not in harmony with American institutions. It is strange that this objection should arise in a land which absorbs half a million of foreigners every year, and which manages to assimilate the very worst elements of continental Europe. It should be remembered that New Mexico was acquired in 1846, that all of its inhabitants except the oldest were born on American soil, and that its people belonged to a sister republic with institutions similar to ours, and so needed no new education in free government. For almost half a century they have been electing their legislatures, making their laws, and carrying on their local government under the American system.

The people have shown themselves as loyal as any in the nation. During the rebellion out of her total population of 93,567 she sent 6,561 into the army. Her volunteers fought at Valverde, Peralta and on other fields; and at Glorieta, together with their comrades of Colorado, defeated the enemy and turned back the column which was advancing northerly from Texas with the intention of cutting off the Pacific Slope from the remainder of the country. The value of that service to the Union cause can scarcely be overestimated. The total number of volunteers from the Territories now composing the six new States of North Dakota, South Dakota, Washington, Montana,

Idaho, and Wyoming was 1,170. Colorado sent but 4,903, and Nebraska, Oregon and Nevada, taken together, did not contribute but 6,047, being 500 less than New Mexico alone.

If we look at the foreign element in the population we will find it smaller in New Mexico than anywhere in the country except in certain Southern States. A comparison with Territories recently admitted is instructive in this regard. The figures are those of the census of 1880, which are the latest on this point.

New Mexico contained 7,219 foreign-born inhabitants to 100,000 native-born, or 7 to 100.

Washington had 26 foreign to 100 native.
Wyoming had 39 foreign to 100 native.
Montana had 41 foreign to 100 native.
Idaho had 44 foreign to 100 native.
Dakota had 62 foreign to 100 native.

Even in the older States, New York and Michigan had 31 to 100; Massachusetts, 33; Rhode Island, 36; Wisconsin, 44; California, 51, and Minnesota, 52. So that New Mexico looms up as a specially native American community.

But to the uninformed the large number of voters of Spanish descent is looked upon as a grave misfortune. There could not be a greater mistake. It is the possession of that conservative element in connection with the energetic and enterprising American from the east which gives New Mexico her special advantages as a self-governing community over most other Territories. Every one familiar with the far west knows that the principal danger in new communities arises from the unsettled and irresponsible character of much of the population.

The chief danger in a new community comes from this class of men and from the overenthusiasm of others who think that life in the new west is a continual boom, and many a State and Territory has suffered from it. But New Mexico runs no such risk. She has a solid, stable, responsible, and conservative element in her native population, which counteracts the danger. They are attached to the soil and have no thought of leaving. They are identified with the country, and naturally opposed to rash schemes which involve extravagant expense and debt. By themselves they might be too slow and nonprogressive, but mixed with the over-zealous American, they form an admirable combination.

Another objection which has been urged against us is that of

ILLITERACY.

Some years ago there may have been some force in this argument, but it is fast disappearing. In no respect has New Mexico been making such rapid progress as in public education. Even under the crude system which existed before the public school law of 1891, the number of children under instruction had increased in a ratio far in advance of the population. The late census developed the fact that while the population of the Territory increased 28 per cent during the decade from 1880 to 1890, the number of children enrolled in the schools increased 283 per cent or ten times as rapidly. The crowning work of the last legislature was that relative to public education. Under its beneficent provisions the educational system is improving with great rapidity.

It should be remembered that all this has to be done by direct taxation, as we have no school fund whatever. We can not have any until we are admitted as a State. Should you deprive all of the States of their school funds a lamentable condition of affairs would result in many of them. With statehood come the grants of land from the public domain for educational purposes. Being a Territory we have no grants and no fund. It is not our fault, for we have been asking for these for years. If there is any fault about it, it is that of Congress, which has deprived us of this among many other rights that come with statehood. If the educational matter is to be weighed against us, it should be weighed in the direction of giving us Statehood, which will increase our means for public education rather than in depriving us of it.

CONCLUSION.

In every respect in which she can control her own destiny, New Mexico is improving and advancing. Her population and wealth are increasing. Railroads are reaching every section. The products of agriculture and horticulture, of the sheep range and the mines, are all enlarged. Great systems of modern irrigation are multiplying her fruitful acreage. The incubus of the past, the uncertainty of land titles, is being removed by the new land court. Wholesome and beneficent legislation is adding to the general prosperity.

Thus in every way the tendency is upward and onward. The sole obstacle to rapid advancement is the continued Territorial condition. It is impossible to obtain money for needed development in a Territory. Eastern capitalists will not loan or invest, as they have an idea that there is no stability of government or security for property without Statehood. To a certain extent immigration is also retarded. It is apt to be thought that a Territory is backward and nonprogressive. The admission of New Mexico into the Union will give a great impetus to its prosperity. Population will flow in with rapidity. The capital wanted for the development of our resources will be easily obtained. Rates of interest will be lowered. We will be relieved from certain Congressional statutes which now impede our progress. The people will feel that they are really American citizens, and not aliens or servants. All this will enkindle ambition, invigorate our energies, stimulate enterprise, and lead us on to a glorious future.

L. BRADFORD PRINCE,
Governor of New Mexico.

CHAPTER XIV.

CONGRESSIONAL—1895 TO 1901.

In the 54th Congress Mr. Joseph was succeeded by Hon. Thomas B. Catron. Mr. Catron had always been an active frined of Statehood and he lost no time in introducing an Enabling Act in the usual form. This was on December 6th, 1895, and the bill was designated "House Bill 219." On account of some clerical errors, the bill was re-introduced on December 9th, with the necessary corrections. The material changes from the more recent Joseph bills, were in an increase in the number of delegates to the Constitutional Convention to 81, the apportionment being made in the bill; greater liberality as to donations of land for public use; and a provision granting the "Palace" in Santa Fe, with all appurtenant lands, to the new State.

Mr. Catron devoted his characteristic energy to the passage of the bill, but was met by the usual delays and the opposition of eastern influences, which at that time, owing to the antagonism between the supporters of a single gold standard and the advocates of bimetalism, were strongly averse to the creation of more western States.

The history of the struggle during the last fifteen years is within the memory of most of those interested in the subject, and presents a succession of attempts, regularly begun at the opening of each new Congress, carried on with more or less vigor, with apparent excellent prospects of success, usually resulting in the passage of the bill by the House of Representatives and its reference in the Senate to the Committee on Territories. Sometimes there would be public hearings by the committee of the Senate or the House; usually the delegate would make at least one speech on the floor of the House, begging for tardy justice to his people; occasionally there would be a few other speeches, more than likely in opposition, and full of uncomplimentary remarks on the Territory and its people. From time to time, the people of the Territory would be told that a demonstration in the form of a Statehood Convention, or the passage of strong resolutions, would be of benefit, by showing public opinion; or that a committee coming to Washington would do good; and they would hasten to carry out the suggested programme as far as possible.

Any one consulting the files of territorial journals for almost any year since 1890, will be surprised to observe the similarity, year after year, in the reports from Washington, and in the general tone of articles on the subject. Statehood has constantly been on the eve of being realized. If it was not obtained that year, it could not fail to come within the next year, or within two years at the farthest. Occasionally there would be some episode which would add to the general interest, and for the time bring the Territory into the limelight of national publicity. So it was when Senator Beveridge began his crusade against admission to Statehood. So it was when Senator Quay became its champion and with all the power of his great State and the force and persistence of his character almost achieved a victory.

We will not attempt, then, to cover this period in minute detail. It will be understood that each delegate in turn introduced an Enabling Act, perhaps a half dozen in different forms, and used his best endeavors for success; and that somewhere, at some stage of the procedure, either in the House or in the Senate, either in committee or on the floor, a snag was encountered, and the bill died at the end of the session because it could not overcome the obstacle in time. During all this long period the bill has never been beaten on a vote, there has never been a majority in either House of Congress willing to be recorded as opposed to self government for American citizens; but it has been killed, or rather allowed to die, by indirection.

The reports made against Statehood, whether by a majority or a minority, have usually been made up of excuses rather than arguments, and have indulged in cruel misrepresentations in order to arouse prejudice. The famous Beveridge report is perhaps an exception to this rule, for, while it is most unjust in many of its statements and conclusions, yet it is actually based on a theory as to the admission of new States which is clearly and frankly stated. That theory is given a hearing elsewhere in this volume, with the antagonistic theory of the right of self-government.

The friends of Statehood have never been afraid of a fair argument, but they have feared the unjust and unfounded sentiment, never openly expressed but no less real, which has permeated nearly the whole eastern mind, against giving more power to the west. It was that underlying feeling which for a generation has kept New Mexico out of the Union, and which has been stronger than ever since the newly admitted States of the northwest have shown remarkable political independence. The opinion has been freely expressed on many occasions within the last ten or twelve years, that it was a great mistake to admit Idaho, Montana, Wyoming and Utah, and that if the question of their admission was to arise now instead of when it did, they would not be admitted; and that any further similar mistake must be avoided. Articles in eastern journals, even since the passage of the Statehood bill for New Mexico and Arizona in June, 1910, have expressed the same feeling, and thus show that the final passage of the Act was rather the result of a fortunate accident than the real intention of the representatives of the east.

The existence of this feeling, strong yet unexpressed, effective though never apparent, must be constantly borne in mind, in order to understand the regular failure, year after year, of the attempts for Statehood, when everything on the surface appeared favorable.

Mr. Catron was succeeded as delegate by Hon. H. B. Fergusson in the 55th Congress, and he, by Hon. Pedro Perea in the 56th. The usual bills for the admission of the three remaining Territories were promptly introduced, and urged by their respective delegates with vigor.

Mr. Fergusson made a strong plea before the Committee on Territories of the House, for New Mexico; and in addition to the usual arguments made a special point regarding the public lands, the immediate necessities of the public schools and other educational institutions, and the danger that by protracted delay all the best of the lands would be taken up by private individuals and lost to the new State.

As usual, the bill failed to become a law, but Congress was sufficiently impressed by the argument as to the public lands to pass an Act giving the Territory a considerable proportion of the areas usually appropriated to new States for the immediate use of the territorial institutions, before admission.

Mr. Perea's term presented nothing noticeably different from that which had become the ordinary routine of endeavor and effort and failure. Like his predecessors, he was an earnest friend of Statehood; but the dominant feeling of Congress was as above described, and controlled in the result.

This brings us to 1901 and the beginning of the last decade of the long struggle. But before taking up that period in its order, the action of the Beveridge committee and movements in the Territory itself, require attention.

CHAPTER XV.

THE BEVERIDGE COMMITTEE.

Pursuant to Senate Resolution No. 282, adopted June 27, 1902, a sub-committee of the Committee on Territories of the Senate assembled at Chicago on November 10, 1902, and proceeded to New Mexico, Arizona, Oklahoma, and the Indian Territory for the purpose of investigating conditions relative to the admission of those Territories to Statehood. The sub-committee was composed of Senator Beveridge (chairman), Senator Dillingham, Senator Burnham and Senator Heitfeld; Senator Heitfeld joining the party en route before reaching New Mexico.

This committee held sessions in this Territory at Las Vegas, Santa Fe, Albuquerque, Las Cruces and Carlsbad, commencing on Wednesday, November 12th, and ending on November 21st. This investigation was not in the form usual in hearings before committees in Washington, where voluntary statements are received from those in attendance, but was rather in the form of a legal proceeding in which witnesses were called and sworn and then testified in answer to questions from the members of the committee. A large number of witnesses were thus examined on particular points as to which the committee desired to obtain information, and the witnesses themselves were selected and summoned by the committee with the exception of a very few who were produced at the request of Delegate Rodey.

The following is a list of the witnesses who were examined during the investigation:

At Las Vegas—
  Judge Wm. J. Mills, Chief Justice.
  Nepomuceno Segura, Court Interpreter.
  Wm. E. Gortner, Court Stenographer.
  Secundino Romero, District Court Clerk.
  Miss Georgia Murray, teacher.
  Miss Francisca Zana, teacher.
  Enrique Armijo, teacher.

Enrique H. Salazar, editor "El Independiente."
Jesus Maria Tafoya, Justice of the Peace.
Pablo Ulibarri, Census Enumerator.
Timoteo Sena, Census Enumerator.
Jose Lino Rivera, Census Enumerator.
H. S. Wooster, Justice of the Peace.
Eugenio Rudolph, Census Enumerator.
Pablo Jaramillo, Census Enumerator.
F. O. Blood, Postmaster.
Rafael Gallegos, Census Enumerator.
Miss Maggie J. Bucher, Superintendent City Schools.
Felipe Baca y Garcia, Justice of the Peace.
Cleofes Romero, Sheriff.

At Santa Fe—
J. Francisco Chaves, Supt. of Public Instruction.
Judge John R. McFie, Judge Supreme Court.
Miss Barbara Perea Yrisarri, Census Enumerator.
Jose D. Sena, Court Interpreter.
Facundo Ortiz, Census Enumerator.
Clemente P. Ortiz, Census Enumerator.
Ambrosio Ortiz, Census Enumerator.
Joseph P. Conklin, Census Enumerator.
James D. Hughes, Publisher.
Francisco Anaya, Justice of the Peace.
A. M. Bergere, District Court Clerk.
Chas. M. Conklin, Justice of the Peace.
Jose Maria Garcia, Justice of the Peace.
Camilo Padilla, Census Enumerator.
Juvencio Quintana, Justice of the Peace.
Leonardo Duran, Justice of the Peace.
Paul A. F. Walter, Postmaster.
Pedro Sanchez, Census Enumerator.

At Albuquerque—
Judge Benj. S. Baker, Supreme Court Judge.
Nestor Montoya, Court Interpreter.
G. W. Metzger, Census Enumerator.
Seferino Crollott, Census Enumerator.
Modesto C. Ortiz, Census Enumerator.
Eslavio Vigil, Census Enumerator.

Wm. Borchert, Justice of the Peace.
A. J. Crawford, Police Judge.
Wm. J. Oliver, Indian School.
C. F. Myers, Mayor.
Thos. Hughes, Editor "Citizen."
Wm. B. Childers, U. S. Attorney.
C. M. Foraker, U. S. Marshal.
Abran Abeytia, County Treasurer.
James A. Summers, Probate Clerk.
W. E. Dame, Court Clerk.
Anastacio C. Torres, School Superintendent.
H. G. Baca, Probate Clerk.
A. A. Sedillo, Court Interpreter.
Chas. P. Newhall, Tax Collector.
Prof. Wm. Geo. Tight, President, University.
Chas. E. Hodgin, Professor, University.
Atanacio Montoya, Teacher.
Hon. B. S. Rodey, Delegate in Congress.
O. N. Marron, Mayor.
Willard S. Hopewell, Cattle, Mines and Railroad.
M. E. Hickey, School Superintendent.

At Las Cruces—
Judge Frank W. Parker, Supreme Court Judge.
Manuel Lopez, Justice of the Peace.
Jose Gonzales, Editor "Labrador."
Samuel A. Steele, Census Enumerator.
Eugene Van Patten, Census Enumerator.
Isidor Armijo, Probate Clerk.
F. D. Hunt, Editor "Progress."
Marcel Valdez, Editor "Tiempo."
Francis E. Lester, College Registrar.
Allen J. Papen, Editor "Republican."
Elias E. Day, School Superintendent.
Martin Amador, Farmer.
John J. Vernon, College Professor.
Martin Lohman, Merchant.

At El Paso—
Judge Daniel H. McMillan, District Court Judge.

At Carlsbad—
Francis Tracy, Irrigation Superintendent.

L. O. Fullen, Editor "Argus."
James O. Cameron, Attorney.
Wm. C. Reiff, Census Enumerator.
R. W. Tansill, Retired Manufacturer.

The arrival of the members of the committee, without notice, at the various points where it held sessions; their method of procedure, which was with closed doors, one witness being admitted at a time; the fact that they came provided with lists of the witnesses whom they desired, and did not hear others, and that they avoided calling many of the most intelligent and well-informed citizens who were close at hand; that their investigation was not as to the resources and industries of the Territory, or its financial condition and ability to bear the expense of Statehood; and that their inquiries, so far as they became known, were nearly all as to the use of Spanish in the courts, in the schools, in the houses and the streets; all these things aroused a strong feeling against the committee and its chairman.

The character of the report based on this testimony was such as to increase the vexation and indignation of the people. It was believed that an adverse report had been agreed on long before the committee visited New Mexico, and that the testimony was taken simply to justify such a report. It was felt that the worst side of every scene, and worst construction of every statement of the witnesses, was that which was presented and emphasized. For a considerable time Senator Beveridge was the most cordially disliked man in New Mexico. The newspapers were filled with articles censuring his course, and every public speech was full of denunciation.

Even the rhymesters made him the target of their humor, as these verses, the first and last of a long "Plea for Statehood," dated December 8th, 1902, will prove:

"Oh, Bevy, ln the name of God,
Withhold, withhold, thy chastening rod.
We implore this on our bended knees,
Give us Statehood, Please do! please!!

If you'd lie down to pleasant dreams,
Not disturbed by our eagle's screams,
Then let us into the Union, pray!
At least, dear boy, get out of the way."

There can be no doubt that at that time he was strongly prejudiced against the Territory and its people, and was determined that it should not be admitted as a State.

The report was presented in the Senate on December 10th, 1902, and ortered printed, with the accompanying exhibits and testimony. (Senate Report No. 2206, 57th Congress, 2nd Session; and Document 36).

It was very carefully drawn, with an evident desire to appear fair, but it approached the subject from a thoroughly eastern point of view, and the following extracts will show that it presented the worst phases of the situation which the testimony taken made possible.

"The great majority of the New Mexican population are native New Mexicans, of Spanish and mixed Spanish and Indian descent, and of these all speak Spanish in the affairs of daily life and the majority speak nothing but Spanish." (p. 5.)

"Courts are conducted through the medium of an interpreter, and it is impossible to conduct the machinery of justice without this official." (p. 5.)

"Coming to the justices of the peace—practically all of them speak Spanish and the proceedings of their courts are conducted in Spanish. The dockets of nearly all justices of the peace are kept almost exclusively in Spanish." (p. 6.)

"Until recently (historically speaking) no English was taught in the public schools. At present both Spanish and English are taught in the most of the schools." (p. 6.)

"In some schools Spanish is taught exclusively; and history, arithmetic and geography are translated from American texts into Spanish." (p. 6.)

"In the little country settlements the people are usually bunched together, their occupation being principally that of herding sheep or goats, and with little or practically no communication with the outside world." (p. 7.)

"A portion of the population, even including some justices of the peace, have little understanding of our institutions." (p. 7.)

"Of the entire population of New Mexico thirty-three and two-tenths per cent. are illiterate; that is, that portion can neither read nor write Spanish, English, or any other language. If the test of illiteracy were confined to the English language only, the committee is of opinion that the percentage of illiterates would be much more than doubled." (p. 7.)

"Even members of grand and pettit juries sometimes sign their names by their mark, and the testimony shows an instance where nineteen out of twenty-one jurors signed by their mark, and another instance of twenty-one out of twenty-four who signed by their mark." (p. 8.)

"As to educational progress, and especially advance in the speaking of English, the committee, after having made every possible allowance, are of the opinion that the very most that can be said is that New Mexico is beginning to get a fair start, and no more." (p. 8.)

"Aside from the large towns, practically all development is Mexican. The Mexican population universally live in adobe or mud houses, just as they did a hundred years ago. Even in the Capital City of Santa Fe practically all the residences and most of the schools are in these earth structures." (p. 9.)

"On the whole, the committee feel that in the course of time, when education, now only practically beginning, shall have accomplished its work; when the mass of the people, or even a majority of them shall, in the usages and employment of their daily life, have become identical in language and customs with the great body of the American people; when the immigration of English speaking people who have been citizens of other States does its modifying work with the Mexican element; when all these things have come to pass, the committee hopes and believes that this mass of people, unlike us in race, language and social customs, will finally come to form a creditable portion of American citizenship." (p. 9.)

"Many of the people of New Mexico do not want Statehood. The testimony of Martin Amador, a Mexican farmer, proves this. The committee is further convinced that this opposition to Statehood for New Mexico is by no means confined to this simple Mexican farmer (Martin Amador) and the great class for whom he spoke. It is true that no other rancher, farmer, or merchant appeared before the committee to the same effect; but the committee has sound reasons for believing that large numbers of them are earnestly against the proposition of New Mexico Statehood."
(p. 29.)

While the statements appearing in these extracts may not be literally untrue, yet they represent extreme and exceptional cases which give an entirely false idea of the average condition of affairs, and are essentially misleading as representing the Territory and people at large.

The underlying fallacy in the argument of the report is that it entirely ignores the fundamental right of the American citizen to self-government, when such government is possible; and, in direct contradiction to facts, it asserts that there is no real deprivation of self government but that it exists practically as in the States.

As the Beveridge report presents this subject in clear-cut form, in direct antagonism to the view held by the people of New Mexico, and has been as distinctly answered on behalf of the Territory before another Committee of Congress, it may be well to present the two sides of the argument in a separate chapter, as this is really the crucial question in controversy between the advocates of Statehood and its opponents in Congress.

CHAPTER XVI.

THE RIGHT TO SELF GOVERNMENT.

It is not proposed to interrupt the course of this narrative of the Struggle for Statehood by a chapter of newly written arguments; but simply to show by a few extracts what has been the real essential issue between the advocates of Statehood and its opponents, as presented to Congress.

THE ARGUMENT AGAINST STATEHOOD.

Senator Beveridge, in his celebrated report, in 1902, formulated the argument against Statehood in the most logical shape in which it has been stated.

He enumerated the necessary qualifications of a community for Statehood as follows:

QUALIFICATIONS.

The people must be sufficient in number; they must be on an equality with the remainder of the people of the nation in all that constitutes effective citizenship; they must have devdloped the resources of the laud they occupy and have further resources susceptible of like development, to bring their proposed new State up to the average of the remainder of the Nation. (p. 2.)

RULE AS TO POPULATION.

It would have been well and would now be well if the rule could be adopted that any new State should have a population equal to the average population of the remainder of the States. This rule would require a population for any proposed new State, at the present time, of 1,650,000." (p. 4.)

OTHER QUALIFICATIONS.

"But not only are numbers of people requisite. The advancement of that people, their state of life, their familiarity and sympathy with our institutions, their educational conditions, and all of the elements that go to make up good citizenship, are to be equally considered. So are the resources of their Territory and the present development of those resources." (p. 5.)

STATEHOOD A REWARD.

"Statehood should come as the reward of development, and not as its inducement. Development and population should precede Statehood, and not the reverse." (p. 22.)

SELF GOVERNMENT.

'This compels consideration of a much-used argument that the people of a Territory are deprived of self-government, and are entitled as a right to this great privilege. This argument is refuted by the fact that the people of the Territories enjoy practically all of the substance of self government that the people of the States enjoy, save only the power of creating unlimited debt. In other respects the people are self-governing; they have their own legislature which they themselves elect. This legislature passes all, or practically all, laws which a State legislature may pass. Their taxes are fixed and levied by themselves. Their schools are established and maintained by themselves. Their crimes and rights are determined, punished and enforced by themselves. Their governors are appointed by the President of the United States, but under the practice now established this governor is always one of themselves; and no administration would, at this day in the Republic's history, keep in office a governor seriously distasteful to a majority of the people." (p. 22.)

THE ANSWERING ARGUMENT FOR SELF GOVERNMENT.

(This is taken from the printed proceedings of the H. R. Committee on Territories Jan. 29, 1908.)

On January 29, 1908, before the House Committee on Territories, Hon. E. L. Hamilton, chairman, Gov. Prince of New Mexico, presented the following resolutions of the Trans-Mississippi Congress, passed November 21, 1907.

"Whereas, self-government is the foundation of republican institutions and the dearest right of every American citizen, and no American community should be deprived of this right except under circumstances which make its exercise impossible, and such deprivation should cease the moment those circumstances come to an end;

"And whereas the people of New Mexico have been kept under a military or Territorial government for over sixty years, although for a long period they have possessed every requisite for successful statehood, including population, taxable valuation, resources, and personal character: Therefore

"Resolved, That this long-continued injustice to our fellow-citizens of New Mexico should cease at the earliest moment, and they should receive their proper right to self-government by the admission of New Mexico as a state."

And said: Our persistency in coming here, year after year, asking for the admission of New Mexico as a State, may almost seem to require an apology, but we come in the spirit of these resolutions which declare that this matter of self-government is the fundamental point in Republican institutions, and is the dearest right of an American citizen; and because we feel that a failure to show that persistence in so vital a matter, would be little less than a crime against our American birthright.

It has seemed to us sometimes that most of the committees of Congress do not fully appreciate what the deprivation of the rights of self-government is to an American citizen; and perhaps this is not entirely unnatural, because, in looking over the membership of this committee, I see that there is only one man on the committee who has ever lived in a territory (Mr. Davenport of Oklahoma.)

The next youngest State which has a member on this committee ended its territorial existence just seventy years ago; a period as great as the span of a lifetime and double the length of a generation; so that the principal membership of this committee is composed of those who have never experienced what it is in America to be without self-government, because they have never lived where it did not exist.

We are all surrounded by a great number of things the value of which we fail to recognize because we have never been deprived of them. We do not realize the value of the surrounding atmosphere until we are suddenly deprived of air, and find ourselves being smothered to death.

If any of you gentlemen, who have lived in an atmosphere of self-government all your days, so that it seems almost like a part of nature itself, should find yourselves suddenly deprived of it entirely, you would probably better appreciate its value, and would have some idea of that of which your fellow-citizens in the territories are deprived. If the officials of your states were appointed by some power in whose selection you had no voice whatever, you would quickly recognize the change in your situation and your comparatively helpless condition. If, in addition to this, that appointing power was located thousands of miles away so that it could by no possibility have a knowledge of local conditions, and the true character of local men, the situation would be far more intolerable.

The system of provincial government, under which local officials are appointed by a central supreme power, far from the localities affected, has always been bad from the days of Babylon anl Assyria down to the Turkish and Persian empires of our own times. It can not be otherwise, for its fundamental principle is wrong. No matter how well-meaning the appointing power may be, the result is largely the same.

Of course, good men may occasionally be appointed under that system as they are under any other, but the system itself is essentially vicious, for it is impossible for the appointing power to have personal knowledge of requirements and character, and the most unworthy or corrupt officials are those who can afford to expend the most, both in time and money, to prevent its enlightenment, or any reform in administration. While it would seem as if, in America, the redress of such evils ought to be easy, experience has too often shown, not only that the officials thus appointed by some accident of favoritism, are entirely regardless of the people, because they are not responsible to them, but also, that the worse the official, the more ingenuity he develops in intrenching himself in power.

Again, this system is practically the destruction of an enlightened and vigilant public sentiment. We are a practical people here in America, and as a rule we do not cultivate anything unless it has practical value, and when public sentiment cannot be effectively exercised in a practical way, it does not flourish. In no community that is not self-governed can you find a healthy, vigorous and active public sentiment either in the Press or among the people, because it is without power either to effect appointments or removals, or to reform the administration of the government. Thus the whole fiber of good citizenship is weakened.

What we insist upon is that this right to self-government is so fundamental in our institutions that no citizen should be deprived of it except under such peculiar circumstances as render its exercise impossible or dangerous. When a population is so sparse that it is not able to support a local government or that elections are impracticable, one of these exceptional cases occurs, and such a population has to be ruled in some other way and is deprived temporarily of its right to self-government; but the moment the peculiar conditions are removed the disability should vanish with them and the citizen should regain his inherent right.

A territorial condition is an exceptional one, only intended as a temporary expedient, and is in derogation of the civil rights of all the citizens affected thereby; and, as the normal condition of an American citizen is one of self-government, the burden of proof is upon those who desire to continue the abnormal form, and not upon those who insist on the organization of a state.

CHAPTER XVII.

JOINT STATEHOOD MOVEMENT OF 1906.

That the idea of Joint-Statehood for New Mexico and Arizona was distasteful in both territories, there is no doubt. There was good reason for this. It was not caused by any ill feeling in either of the Territories toward the other, but because there was an entire lack of cohesion and community of interest. They were more disconnected, so far as personal acquaintance and business or social relations go, than most States far more distant from each other. Nature itself had separated them by placing the great Continental Divide as a practical barrier between them. The rivers of New Mexico flow eastward or southward to the Gulf of Mexico and the Atlantic; those of Arizona flow westward to the Gulf of California and the Pacific. The trade and business relations of Arizona are with California and the Pacific coast, those of New Mexico are with Kansas City, St. Louis, Chicago, and New York. As a rule no New Mexican visits Arizona except en route to California; and no citizen of Arizona visits New Mexico except en route to the east; and those visits are simply en passant. The number of residents of either Territory who have ever passed a night in the other, except in a railroad car, is remarkably small. In short, there is less connection between the two than there is between either one of them and New York or California.

It seemed impossible for the eastern mind to grasp this elemental fact. The average eastern Congressman, knowing that each Territory was anxious for Statehood, and really unfavorable to an increase of western States, looked at the map, saw two squares contiguous to each other, and instantly found a satisfactory solution of the difficulty by saying: "Why not join them together and make one oblong of them?" The opponents of western influence saw in this an easy method to reduce the danger of too many Senators; and to the ignorant and unthinking it seemed a simple and natural arrangement; and so the "joint Statehood Bill" was passed. How President Roosevelt could have been induced to favor it, with his general knowledge of western conditions, is one of those mysterious things past ordinary comprehension; but he certainly did give the project the entire weight of his great influence.

The feeling on the part of Arizona was plainly expressed. Gov. Joseph H. Kibbey in his report to the Secretary of the Interior, of 1905, devoted almost his entire attention to an argument, and an able one, against jointure, from the Arizona standpoint. He summed up the matter in this brief sentence: "The proposed union is regarded by our people as a menace to the property and progress of the Territory."

At the hearings before the Committee on Territories of the House of Representatives in January, 1906, the representatives of Arizona expressed their opposition to this union—we might almost say, their detestation of it—in words more forcible than complimentary. It would be difficult to use language more distinct. The chairman of their delegation, Mr. Dwight B. Heard, said: "We are opposed to Joint Statehood. We want to be let alone. A vast majority of the people of Arizona, regardless of politics or business, are utterly opposed to Joint Statehood."

Mr. R. E. Morrison said: "We object to this amalgamation, and object to being dominated by people whom we do not think should be mixed up with us at all."

They presented a petition against jointure which they stated had been signed by thirty-one hundred people within thirty minutes, at their Territorial Fair; and they added that only two per cent. of those to whom it was then presented declined to sign.

Mr. W. S. Sturges said: "I know the Arizona cattle men; every one, owner and cow boy, is against Joint Statehood to a finish. As one man expressed it, 'We would rather see it a Territory to all eternity than joined to New Mexico.'"

Gen. A. J. Sampson used these words: "It would be unwise, unjust and un-American to force us into the proposed Statehood." "In the name of all that is just and right do not try to force us into this unnatural, inharmonious, unholy and un-American wedlock."

More than a dozen members of that delegation addressed the committee and each in turn said that while they wished for Statehood, yet they infinitely preferred remaining as a Territory to being linked with New Mexico.

While no such violent language was used in New Mexico, yet the general sentiment of the people of the Territory was thoroughly opposed to jointure.

What made the plan even more unpalatable to New Mexicans was the proposition to call the new State "Arizona." This showed as great an ignorance of history as the proposed union did of geography.

For Arizona at best only represented what had been a single county of New Mexico, and to impose the name of the daughter on the parent domain, was, at least, a humiliation. Besides, the name Arizona had no settled meaning and no historic interest. It seems, according to the best authorities, to have been the Pima name of the locality of a mine in northern Sonora, with no known significance and very various spelling; and was used as a name of a new county established by the New Mexico legislature in 1860 to include the Gadsden Purchase and adjoining territory. To abandon the historic name of New Mexico was always obnoxious to the New Mexican people, for reasons stated in another chapter.

But the Joint Statehood Bill having been passed and signed, the practical question was, what to do about it. The national administration in Washington was fully committed to this plan of admission. The Territories were practically threatened by the dominant powers at the national Capitol that if this plan for admission was rejected by the people, it would be long before any new opportunity for Statehood could be obtained. In the minds of most New Mexicans it was a choice between two evils, and the intense desire to escape from the demoralizing conditions almost inseparable from the provincial system, and to enjoy the American right of self-government, prevailed with a great number of citizens.

Mr. Rodey stated his own change of opinion and the reasons therefor very plainly before the House Committee on January 20th, 1906. He said: "It is either Joint Statehood now or else it is a Territorial condition for twenty years to come." "It is my firm and absolute belief that New Mexico and Arizona will never come into the Union except as a Joint State, and we might as well come to it now as at any other time." "Three years ago I was shocked at the idea of jointure. But we have found that separate Statehood in modern times is impossible."

The two political organizations in New Mexico, usually too antagonistic to work harmoniously in any cause, through their territorial committees united in an appeal to the people to vote "aye" at the election, for Joint Statehood. In their joint circular they said: "President Roosevelt has frankly told us that if we reject this offer we must expect years to pass before we have another. He has asked us to accept it. We believe this is true." "If the people of Arizona see fit to reject it, however much we may regret it, that is no reason why New Mexico should do so. A decided vote for it by New Mexico will undoubtedly hasten the day when we will get Statehood, either joint or single." Then follows a full statement as to the donations of public lands, their aid to the public schools, etc., and the circular signed by the ten members of the joint committee, concluded with these stirring words: "And we appeal to every citizen in New Mexico to aid by his vote in securing this splendid provision for the education of the children of the State, representation in Congress and full rights of American citizens for all our people."

It is probable that the almost universal belief that Arizona would vote against jointure, and that consequently New Mexico could show her desire for Statehood without danger, and place herself in a favorable position for future action in Washington, had influence with some. At all events, the majority in favor of admission under the Joint Statehood Act, at the election of 1906, in New Mexico, was a very substantial one, the vote being nearly two to one in the Territory and as high as ten to one in certain counties. It was officially announced as follows:

CANVASS OF VOTE BY COUNTIES ON JOINT STATEHOOD QUESTION.

County.	Yes.	No.
Bernalillo	2623	1087
Chaves	1279	308
Colfax	2177	793
Dona Ana	1512	290
Eddy	871	278
Grant	980	696
Guadalupe	611	608
Lincoln	519	500
Luna	207	170
McKinley	259	89
Mora	1606	394
Otero	795	351
Quay	572	267
Rio Arriba	676	2038
Roosevelt	1020	91
Sandoval	518	438
San Juan	763	122
San Miguel	2503	1688
Santa Fe	697	1447
Sierra	307	418
Socorro	2040	455
Taos	822	1070
Torrance	551	275
Union	705	731
Valencia	1582	122
	26195	14735

Majority for Joint Statehood 11,460

The following were the delegates elected in New Mexico to the Constitutional Convention:

Bernalillo County—Federico Chaves, F. W. Clancy, T. R. Duran, G. S. Klock, E. S. Stover.

Chaves County—J. W. Poe, G. A. Richardson.

Colfax County—M. M. Dawson, P. G. Santistevan, Charles Springer, Jerome Troy.

Dona Ana County—L. F. Elliot, Jose Gonzales, R. E. McBride.

Eddy County—E. P. Bujac.

Grant County—J. L. Burnside, T. W. Carter, R. P. Thompson.

Guadalupe County—Celso Baca, F. B. Morse.

Lincoln County—J. Y. Hewitt, G. W. Prichard.

Luna County—J. N. Upton.

McKinley County—Edward Hart.

Mora County—C. Fernandez, Frank A. Roy, Blas Sanchez, G. P. Sanchez.

Otero County—J. M. Helm, J. L. Lawson.

Quay County—C. C. Davidson.

Rio Arriba County—T. D. Burns, J. M. C. Chaves, E. A. Jaques, L. B. Prince, M. S. Salazar.

Roosevelt County—George L. Reese.

Sandoval County—Manuel Armijo, Paulin Montoya.

San Juan County—Jay Turley.

San Miguel County—Roman Gallegos, Jefferson Raynolds, Margarito Romero, W. R. Tipton, R. E. Twitchell, Enrique Sena, Isidro V. Gallegos.

Santa Fe County—J. W. Akers, T. B. Catron, David M. White, J. A. Wood.

Sierra County—H. A. Wolford.

Socorro County—H. O. Bursum, M. Cooney, Porfirio Sanchez, A. A. Sedillo.

Taos County—Jose I. Garcia, Epimenio D. Leon, A. C. Pacheco.

Torrance County—F. A. Zamora.

Union County—O. P. Easterwood, E. Sandoval, M. B. Sisneros.

Valencia County—Higinio Chaves, Manuel P. y Chaves, Boleslo Romero.

Arizona voted "No" on the Joint Statehood proposition, by an overwhelming vote, as had been expected; and that negative vote ended all further proceedings under the Joint Statehood Act.

CHAPTER XVIII.

PROPOSED CONVENTION OF 1907.

With careful foresight preliminary measures had been taken in advance of the election, to take advantage of exactly the situation which actually did occur, by arranging that in case Arizona declined the proffered partnership, but New Mexico voted for Statehood, the New Mexican delegates should meet and formulate a constitution for that State alone, and present it in Washington with a request for admission under it.

The advantages of this course were obvious to everyone informed as to the history of the admission of Territories. Much of the opposition in Congress to the passage of the Enabling Act was founded, either really or as a pretext, on doubts as to the character of Constitution that the Territory would adopt, and this objection would be entirely avoided by presenting the Constitution in advance. The only practical objection to holding such a convention was the fact that, as it was a voluntary meeting not contemplated by the Act of Congress, there would be no salary attached to the service, and the work would be a patriotic labor of love. It was thought, however, that for such an important service, and with the goal of immediate Statehood in view, nearly if not quite all of the delegates elected would be willing to attend.

Looking forward to the desirability of such action, the Republican Territorial Convention held just previous to the election, in Las Vegas, unanimously adopted the following resolution, offered by Hon. L. B. Prince:

"Resolved, That in case the Hamilton Statehood Bill fails to become operative through the adverse vote of the people either of Arizona or New Mexico, we recommend and urge that the 66 delegates elected in New Mexico to the constitutional convention, should assemble in the Capitol on January 7, 1907, and formulate a constitution for the State of New Mexico; and we further urge that the territorial legislature enact a law submitting said constitution to the vote of the people, and if approved by them, providing for its presentation to Congress, with a request for the admission of New Mexico into the Union as a State thereunder."

Precisely the circumstances contemplated by the resolution having arisen, a considerable number of the delegates, representing all sections of the Territory, met at the Capitol in Santa Fe on January 7th, 1907, and organized by the election of L. B. Prince of Rio Arriba County, as president, and David M. White of Santa Fe, as secretary. Letters were received from a large number of absent delegates stating that they would attend as soon an active business was commenced. Letters were also read from a number of leading U. S. Senators expressing great interest in the work of the convention and urging the early formation and presentation of a constitution. The Governors of Colorado, Oregon, Wisconsin, North Dakota and other States sent copies of their constitutions and other documents, with their good wishes. A telegraphic dispatch was received from the President of the Constitutional Convention of Oklahoma, then in session, conveying the greetings of that body, and this was followed up by the resolutions in full, sent by mail and received shortly thereafter as follows:

WHEREAS, the people of Oklahoma earnestly sympathize with the desire of the people of New Mexico for independent statehood,

Therefore, be it resolved, We congratulate the delegates elected by the people of New Mexico upon their determination to draft a constitution for the State of New Mexico, and hereby tender them our cordial sympathy.

We believe that New Mexico is entitled to Statehood as of right; that the denial of Statehood to the people of New Mexico is a serious wrong.

We believe that the denial of Statehood to New Mexico would be an injury, not only to the great West, but to the Union itself.

That the president telegraph the greetings of this convention to the New Mexico Constitutional Convention.

JNO. M. YOUNG,   WILLIAM H. MURRAY,
    Secretary.   President.

After a full discussion of the situation, it was resolved to adjourn to February 5th, when the legislature would be in session; and the following resolutions were adopted:

RESOLUTION.

WHEREAS, the delegates elected by the people of New Mexico to the proposed joint constitutional convention of New Mexico and Arizona did on January 7th, 1907, convene and assemble at Santa Fe, New Mexico, for the purpose of drafting an independent constitution for the people of New Mexico, with a view to its submission to Congress with a demand for immediate admission of New Mexico, as a State of the Union.

Whereas, The people of New Mexico have demonstrated their desire for Statehood in the most emphatic manner at the recent election, by giving a vote of 26,195 against 14,735, in favor thereof, under very adverse conditions; and the total vote of over 43,000 cast at that election, proves that the present population of the territory is more than ample for separate New Mexico statehood.

Resolved, That we are willing and ready to perform our part in the preparation of a constitution for New Mexico at such time as shall appear most proper and convenient.

Resolved, by this meeting of delegates duly elected from New Mexico to the Constitutional Convention provided for in the Act of Congress commonly called the Hamilton Bill, that in our opinion the admission of New Mexico as a State can be greatly facilitated and hastened by the adoption of a proper constitution and its presentation to Congress with a request for admission thereunder.

Resolved, That a committee, representing all sections, be appointed to confer with the territorial legislature soon to convene, as to the best time and method of holding the session for the formulation of such constitution, and to take such measures as appear best for the promotion of the object.

At the February meeting, a large number of delegates who could not attend in January, were present. All recognized the importance of framing a constitution as soon as practicable, in order to secure early Congressional action, but there was considerable discussion as to the desirability of asking the legislature to make an appropriation for the necessary expenses of the convention. Many delegates were willing to serve without salary, but recognized the injustice of asking those not pecuniarly able, to pay their expenses in addition to devoting their time to the cause. Mr. Klock wished to pay his own expenses, but Mr. Davidson of Quay County suggested the injustice of that course to delegates having long distances to travel. Mr. Reese of Roosevelt, by letters, agreed with this latter view. Gov. Stover thought that it was only fair to pay necessary expenses and this appeared to be the general opinion. Mr. Catron moved that a committee of seven be appointed to prepare a bill for the legislature, looking to a meeting of the convention in August, and to confer with members of that body relative to its provisions and passage. This committee consisted of Messrs. Catron, Stover, Bursum, Boleslo Romero, G. P. Sanchez, Jose Gonzales and D. M. White.

For reasons difficult to understand, no further action was taken. The legislature was a very busy one and largely occupied by political contentions, and gave the subject scant attention. While the "New Mexican," the Albuquerque "Citizen," and many local papers earnestly supported the plan of forming a constitution, the Las Veags "Optic" and some other journals which apparently thought an enabling act was necessary and did not remember that more than half the Territories had been admitted on their own application without prior action of Congress, opposed the meeting of the convention. After the legislature had failed to act, the Governor was asked to name a time for the assembling of the delegates, in order to give the convention his official sanction, but this also failed.

Thus again the opportunity for almost immediate admission was lost. Every one has since realized that if the delegates had gone on with their work and prepared a constitution, and the matter could thus have been presented to Congress in the succeeding winter, free from uncertainty as to the character of the government which would be established, New Mexico would have become a State in 1908, and in time to vote at the presidential election of that year. What is almost equally important is, that the constitution would have been framed quietly and deliberately, without clamor, coercion or excitement, and would almost certainly have been a model instrument, embodying the best systems founded on modern experience, without the theories which still lack the sanction of practical operation under various conditions.

Before leaving this subject, it is simply just to name the delegates who attended the meetings and showed active interest in the work, together with those who were perhaps equally zealous in the good cause, and promised to attend whenever needed, but did not think it necessary to be present until the real work should be commenced.

Beside President Prince of Rio Arriba County and Secretary White of Santa Fe, they were as follows—taken in their order by counties:

E. S. Stover,
F. W. Clancy,
G. S. Klock,
Jose Gonzales,
Celso Baca,
F. D. Morse,
G. W. Prichard,
Edward Hart,
C. Fernandez,
G. P. Sanchez,
C. C. Davidson,
J. M. C. Chavez,
E. A. Jaquez,

M. S. Salazar,
G. L. Reese,
Jay Turley,
Margarito Romero,
Jefferson Raynolds,
W. R. Tipton,
T. B. Catron,
J. W. Akers,
H. O. Bursum,
J. I. Garcia,
E. D. Leon,
A. C. Pacheco,
Boleslo Romero,

Mr. Romero, of Valencia, also assured the convention that his two colleagues from that county, would certainly attend when wanted.

CHAPTER XIX.

CONGRESSIONAL ACTION, 1901 TO 1910.

Hon. Bernard S. Rodey was delegate from New Mexico in both the 57th and 58th Congresses, which extended from 1901 to 1905.

To say that he was devoted to the cause of Statehood is to state the case mildly. He was enthusiastically devoted to it. He set before himself as the one great object to be attained during his Conbressional service, the passage of an Enabling Act for New Mexico. Everything else was subordinated to it, in order that this particular matter could have undivided attention.

In Washington and New Mexico, in hotels and on railroad trains, in public speech and in conversation, in season and out of season, this was his one great theme; and nothing could weary him so long as there was an argument to answer or an auditor to convince.

At the very outset of his Congressional work, at the opening of the 57th Congress, he endeavored to arrange with the Speaker so that the New Mexico Statehood bill should be the first introduced in that session, and actually succeeded in having it recorded as House Bill No. 2. The bill, as usual, went to the Committee on Territories.

Unfortunately there was great activity relative to the territories at this session. While but three of the regularly organized territories still existed, each was making heroic efforts to be admitted to the Union and each was selfishly anxious to be the first to receive consideration. Among the Statehood bills then in the Committee on Territories were No. 2, the New Mexico bill just named; No. 152, an Enabling Act for Oklahoma; No. 2015, a similar bill for Arizona; No. 4570, authorizing single Statehood for Oklahoma and Indian Territory; No. 9675, providing for the union of Oklahoma and Indian Territory; No. 11992, another bill for Arizona singly; No. 11995, a similar bill for New Mexico; and No. 12543, "to enable the people of Oklasoma, Arizona and New Mexico to form constitutions and state governments, and be admitted into the Union on an equal footing with the original states."

On April 1, 1902, the committee, through Mr. Knox, reported in favor of the latter measure, thus uniting all the territories in one omnibus bill. (Report No. 1309). In this shape it passed the House on May 9th and was received by the Senate on May 12th.

It was at this stage of the long struggle, that Senator Quay of Pennsylvania became such an ardent champion of New Mexico, that the grateful people through their legislature named one of their counties for him.

From this time as long as he remained in the Senate he was always not only the consistent friend but the outspoken advocate of the Sunshine Territory, and gave its cause in the Senate a power that it never before had possessed. In the very beginning of the second session of this Congress—December, 1902—came the first clash between Senator Quay and Senator Beveridge on the subject of this bill; Senator Beveridge wishing a postponement and Senator Quay urging immediate action. "If we are to have a fight," said the latter, "we may as well have it this afternoon."

The plan of the opponents of New Mexico at this time was to drop New Mexico and Arizona from the bill and pass it for Oklahoma alone.

On December 15th, 1902, Senator Bate presented a minority report signed by himself and Senators. Heitfeld, Bailey and Patterson (Report No. 2206) favoring the passage of the House bill as it stood and ably arguing the cause of New Mexico and opposing its exclusion from the bill. This report quoted at considerable length from a recent speech of Senator Quay.

The discussion continued to the end of the session on March 4th, all attempts to secure a final vote having failed. On February 19th, Senator Elkins made an excellent speech in favor of New Mexico and its people. He spoke from his own experience in the Territory not only of the prevalent conditions and the character of the people, but bore testimony as to the wretched system of Territorial government. "No man who has not lived in a Territory can understand how dwarfing are the conditions that obtain. I lived in New Mexico ten years and I know how intolerable are the burdens of a Territorial government. A Territory is simply a temporary arrangement, a probation period."

The end of the session of course destroyed the hopes of immediate Statehood and left the work to be begun again in the next Congress; and so far as New Mexico was concerned, the history of the 58th Congress was very similar to that of the 57th. Mr. Rodey was equally zealous as in the preceding Congress; but even his enthusiasm could not produce the desired effect; and the sessions were barren of result.

The question of forming one State by uniting New Mexico and Arizona, became prominent at this time, the bill which elicited most debate being H. R. 14749, which was an enabling act for Oklahoma and the Indian Territory as one State, and for New Mexico and Arizona as one State. On this, Senator Beveridge made a notable speech, entitled "Arizona the Great," in closing the discussion on February 6, 1905, in which he pictures the glory of the combined State in these eloquent words: "Not Arizona the little, but Arizona the great; not Arizona the provincial, but Arizona the national; not Arizona the creature of a politician's device, but Arizona the child of the Nation's wisdom."

In 1905, Hon. W. H. Andrews became delegate from New Mexico, and took up the work of the Struggle where it had been left by his predecessor. Mr. Andrews was no less anxious for Statehood than Mr. Rodey; but his method of operation was entirely different. He was never known to make a regular "speech," except of the shortest description; but as a quiet and convincing conversationalist he had few equals. From long experience in legislative bodies he had learned that quiet, individual work is the most effective, and he employed this method assiduously. His close connection with Senators Quay and Penrose and the Pennsylvania delegation gave him an influence that was very valuable, and which was constantly used to advance the cause of New Mexican statehood.

On December 13th, 1905, Mr. Andrews introduced H. R. 7042, an Enabling Act with the usual title, which took the customary course of reference to the Committee on Territories. Soon afterwards, on January 20, 1906, Mr. Hamilton, chairman of the committee, presented a bill quite similar to the one discussed during the preceding session, to enable Oklahoma and the Indian Territory to become one State, and New Mexico and Arizona another; and this passed the House almost immediately, on January 25th. At the opening of the second session of this Congress (the 59th) Senator Teller introduced a bill for separate Statehood for New Mexico (Senate 7079) ; the jointure project having been rejected by the vote of Arizona in November; and as there was no chance for action at that time, he re-introduced the same bill at the beginning of the next Congress on December 4, 1907, (Senate 515, 60th Congress).

Two days before, on December 2nd, the first day of the session, Delegate Andrews introduced a single Statehood bill for New Mexico, in the usual form (House Bill No. 4). At his request Senator Penrose presented the same bill in the Senate on December 9th (Senate 1484). It was on this House bill that the hearing was held on January 29, 1908, referred to elsewhere. Practically the same bill was re-introduced at the beginning of the short session of that Congress, December 8th, 1908; as that was the time when action had been promised a year before by certain officials in Washington; but as usual that promise turned out to be only a subterfuge for delay.

On February 3rd, 1909, Hon. E. L. Hamilton, of Michigan, chairman of the House Committee, who deserves a warm spot in the heart of every New Mexican on account of his constant friendliness to the Territory, introduced House Bill No. 27607 of the 60th Congress, being an enabling act for New Mexico and one for Arizona, combined in one bill, but entirely separate in their operations. This was the conclusion of the House Committee on the subject of Statehood for the Territories, after various hearings and full consideration during the greater part of two sessions of Congress; and was as satisfactory to New Mexico as could be expected. Of course it could not be passed in the few remaining weeks of that Congress, but it presented a good foundation for work and success in the succeeding year.

When the 61st Congress met, in December, 1909, Mr. Andrews again represented New Mexico, having been reelected mainly on the Statehood issue. He pursued the course of wisdom by co-operating with the House Committee on Territories, with the result that on January 17, 1910, the so-called Hamilton Bill—H. R. 18166—was passed by the House of Representatives without opposition. It was received in the Senate the next day and referred to the Committee on Territories.

It was well known that Senator Beveridge had in mind a number of provisions varying from those in the Hamilton Bill, and his ideas took official shape in a bill introduced in the Senate on January 31, by Senator Dillingham "for Mr. Beveridge" who was absent from Washington. This bill, known as Senate 5916, had exactly the same title as that of the Hamilton Bill, and was immediately referred to the same committee.

Thanks to strong influences outside of Congress, preeminent among which was that of President Taft, who insisted that the pledge contained in the Republican National Platform should be fulfilled by the admission of the Territories, there was now little outspoken opposition to Statehood for either New Mexico or Arizona; and the Senate Committee, having both bills before it, was in a position to settle all details. Various hearings were held, including that of February 18th, referred to in another Chapter, and the committee gave careful attention to the subject until March 14th, when Mr. Beveridge made a report, using the Hamilton Bill (H. R. 18166) as its basis, but striking out all of that bill and substituting the Beveridge bill with a few slight amendments.

This report put the bill on the calendar as No. 388,

and brought the matter squarely before the Senate. Good faith and good temper characterized the final disposition of this great subject.

CHAPTER XX.

FINAL SUCCESS.

For three months the Statehood Bill remained on the calendar of the Senate, and until June 15th there was always a doubt as to the final result. As time passed Congress became restless at the length of the session, and the members expressed great anxiety for an adjournment not later than Saturday, June 18th. Several times the consideration of the Statehood Bill had been postponed in order to allow other measures of national importance to be taken up, and the last of these was what was known as the Conservation Bill. While the action of the Committee on Territories appeared to be in good faith, yet there were still many who were suspicious of its real desire for the passage of the bill.

At length, on June 15th, at half past five in the afternoon, the Conservation Bill was passed; the Statehood Bill was immediately announced, and as the hour was late, by general agreement it was made "unfinished business," which would bring it up at two p. m. on every day until finally disposed of; and the Senate then adjourned.

On the succeeding day at exactly two o'clock Vice-President Sherman laid the Statehood Bill before the Senate as the subject then in order. Senator Beveridge as chairman of the Committee on Territories, explained the proposed amendments embodied in the Senate Bill. The most important was that which required the Statehood elections in Arizona to be held under the territorial law as it existed before the disfranchising statute of the last legislature; others related to the donations of public lands, to the payment of territorial and local debts, etc.

He was followed by Senators Frazier, Nelson, Hughes and Smoot. All were in favor of Statehood, but the democratic Senators preferred the Hamilton or House Bill. Senator Frazier, speaking for the democrats on the committee, opposed the Senate substitute because it sought to fix the qualifications of voters in Arizona. Senator Hughes also advocated the House Bill because it did not place so many restrictions on the new States as were contained in the Senate Bill. Senator Smoot insisted on immediate admission and said that even if both new States were to be democratic he would favor their admission as a right.

The only division was as to preference for the Senate or the House Bill. The vote on this question was by strict party lines, the republicans voting for the Senate Bill and the democrats for the House Bill, the result being 42 to 19 in favor of the former. On the final vote on the passage of the bill, the vote was unanimous!

While this result was extremely gratifying, there was still much apprehension felt as to the result in case the House declined to concur in the Senate amendments and insisted on a conference. The latter was the usual course of procedure, and it was freely asserted that the two Houses would never agree. In fact, it was intimated that the action of the Senate would not have been so harmonious but for the general belief that the House would nonconcur.

Here again the President did good service to New Mexico. He held conferences with several influential members of the House, including Chairman Hamilton, and urged that the Senate amendments should be concurred in without conference. His influence was very effective, and many who preferred the House Bill agreed to sink their personal desires in order to avoid any risk as to the final passage of the bill. The President was also anxious to have early action in order that the bill might be signed before his contemplated journey to the Yale Commencement on Monday, the 20th. Another factor that contributed to this action was the desire for an early adjournment of Congress, and the certainty that a conference, followed by a disagreement, would bring about a long debate that would greatly retard the close of the session.

Mr. Andrews, upon whose judgment many relied, concluded that now that success was actually within its grasp, it was better for the Territory to accept the Senate amendments and end the matter forever, than to run any risk of failure through a disagreement of the Houses. Governor Mills, who was in Washington at the time, concurred in this view and telegraphed on the 17th that the House would probably accept the action of the Senate. On that day the bill still lay on the table of the Speaker, not yet announced.

Shortly after two o'clock on the afternoon of Saturday, June 18th, Speaker Cannon laid the bill as amended in the Senate before the House. There was a moment of suppressed excitement, and then Mr. Lloyd of Missouri, the senior democratic member of the committee, rose and said that while he was not entirely satisfied with the Senate Bill, yet in order to insure immediate Statehood for the Territories he would not oppose it. Instantly, Mr. Hamilton, the committee chairman, moved to concur in the Senate amendments. Shouts of "vote, vote," arose from all sides of the House. The question was put, viva voce, there being no demand for a roll call, and the House concurred by a unanimous vote!

The deed was done! The long conflict of sixty years was over! Members crowded around Delegate Andrews to offer congratulations. All knew that the passage of this bill had been the object of his labors for years and that this was the happiest moment of his life.

The good news was flashed to Santa Fe, and in a moment by direction of Acting Governor Jaffa, the national flag was unfurled on the tall staff at the corner of the historic Palace, and following the lead of the "New Mexican," where the news was first received, all the buildings on the Plaza were quickly covered with red, white and blue.

AT LAST.

That was on Saturday.

The President had signified his desire to affix the signature which would give legal vitality to the bill and transform it into a Law, before leaving Washington on Monday; so, all the preceding formalities were hastened.

On Monday morning, notwithstanding its length, the Statehood Bill was properly enrolled and ready for the official signatures. As soon as the House assembled it was signed by Speaker Cannon; then it was hurried to the Senate chamber, where the Vice-President affixed his autograph at exactly half past twelve.

From the Capitol it was quickly conveyed to the White House, where the President was ready to act. Here were assembled several of those who had been most active in achieving its success, with such representatives of the two Territories as were in the National Capital. The House Committee was represented by Chairman Hamilton, whose self-abnegation in allowing the Senate Bill to be substituted for his own should not soon be forgotten, and by Representatives Guernsey and Cole. The Senate Committee was appropriately represented by its chairman, Senator Beveridge. Postmaster General Hitchcock, who had rendered efficient aid, represented the Cabinet. Delegate Andrews from New Mexico, and Delegate Cameron from Arizona, the actual representatives of the newly enfranchised commonwealths were prominent, and beside them were Thomas B. Catron, of Santa Fe, H. I. Latham of Phoenix, and J. T. Williams of Tucson, with Ira M. Bond, the well known New Mexican correspondent, and others interested.

The President said a few words of congratulation, and then proposed to affix his official signature. The Postmaster General presented a gold pen, with the request that it should be used, and Delegate Andrews produced the unique gold-banded quill taken from the great American eagle captured in Taos, and furnished for the occasion, in its beautiful case, as a patriotic service by George B. Paxton, when he had no thought that Death would forbid his presence at the ceremony. The President wrote half of the signature with the former and the remainder with the latter; returning the pens to the donors as mementoes of this great historic occasion.

The White House clock stood at 1:40 p. m.

That signature ended the drama of the "Struggle for Statehood." There had been more than fifty Statehood Bills in the sixty years of effort. Those few penstrokes transformed a Statehood Bill into a Statehood Law.

The people of New Mexico were no longer serfs but Freemen; no longer subjects but Citizens; no longer to be treated as aliens but as Americans.

HALLELUJAH!

Sixty-first Congress of the United States of America;

At the Second Session,

Begun and held at the City of Washington on Monday, the sixth day of December, one thousand nine hundred and nine.

AN ACT

To enable the people of New Mexico to form a constitution and state government and be admitted into the Union on an equal footing with the original States; and to enable the people of Arizona to form a constitution and state government and be admitted into the Union on an equal footing with the original States.

Be it enacted by the Senate and House of Representatives of the United States of America in Congress assembled, That the qualified electors of the Territory of New Mexico are hereby authorized to vote for and choose delegates to form a constitutional convention for said Territory for the purpose of framing a constitution for the proposed State of New Mexico. Said convention shall consist of one hundred delegates; and the governor, chief justice, and secretary of said Territory shall apportion the delegates to be thus selected, as nearly as may be, equitably among the several counties thereof in accordance with the voting population, as shown by the vote cast at the election for Delegate in Congress in said Territory in nineteen hundred and eight: *Provided*, That in the event that any new counties shall have been added after said election, the apportionment for delegates shall be made proportionate to the vote cast within the various precincts contained in the area of such new counties so created, and the proportionate number of delegates so apportioned shall be deducted from the original counties out of which such counties shall have been created.

The governor of said Territory shall, within thirty days after the approval of this Act, by proclamation, in which the aforesaid apportionment of delegates to the convention shall be fully specified and announced, order an election of the delegates aforesaid on a day designated by him in said proclamation, not earlier than sixty nor later than ninety days after the approval of this Act. Such election for delegates shall be held and conducted, the returns made, and the certificates of persons elected to such convention issued, as nearly as may be, in the same manner as is prescribed by the laws of said Territory regulating elections therein of members of the legislature existing at the time of the last

Statehood Act of 1910.   First Page.

constitutional convention and the election for the ratification of the constitution, at the same rates that are paid for similar services under the territorial laws, and for the payment of the mileage for and salaries of members of the constitutional convention, at the same rates that are paid to members of the said territorial legislature under national law, and for the payment of all proper and necessary expenses, officers, clerks, and messengers thereof, and printing and other expenses incident thereto: *Provided,* That any expense incurred in excess of said sum of one hundred thousand dollars shall be paid by said State. The said money shall be expended under the direction of the Secretary of the Interior, and shall be forwarded to be locally expended in the present Territory of Arizona, through the secretary of said Territory, as may be necessary and proper in the discretion of the Secretary of the Interior, in order to carry out the full intent and meaning of this Act.

J G Cannon
Speaker of the House of Representatives.

J S Sherman
Vice-President of the United States and
President of the Senate.

Approved
Wm H Taft
June 20 1910
in duplicate

Statehood Act of 1910. Last Page.

www.ingramcontent.com/pod-product-compliance
Lightning Source LLC
Chambersburg PA
CBHW020803160426
43192CB00006B/427